Praise for

the referral

"Businesses spend thousands on marketing and advertising, yet frequently overlook the greatest potential source for new business leads: their existing relationships. *The Referral Code* lays out a simple, highly effective system for motivating your clients, friends and associates to connect you with the people they know who need what you offer."

— Daniel H. Pink, author of *Drive* and *A Whole New Mind*

"Guerrilla marketers know that the best source of new customers is old customers and that the way to tap into that source is referrals. That's exactly why Larry Pinci and Phil Glosserman wrote *The Referral Code* and why you'll love it."

— Jay Conrad Levinson, Author, "Guerrilla Marketing" series of books

"Most professionals want more referrals, but don't understand what it really takes to get them. There are two keys to generating massive referrals: 1) a system that works, and 2) the guts to take action. *The Referral Code* will give you the system and plenty of inspiration to take action. Read it and reap!"

— Tim O'Brien, President of The Personal Branding Group
and author of *The Power of Personal Branding*

"*The Referral Code* system not only unlocked a constant stream of business for me, it opened up a floodgate. It's by far the best warm-lead generator I have ever experienced. I've been in the insurance business for over 20 years and I received more referrals in 60 days of using this system than I have in any year."

— John Moore, Vice President, Lockton Companies

"At first I thought this was going to be just a bunch of mumbo jumbo, but damn if this Referral Code stuff doesn't work. I used these techniques with some of my clients yesterday and got referrals every time!"

— Doug Oakley, Sr. Sales Executive, Bald Head Island, Ltd.

"The people you know have the ability to refer you business, but most people won't do it on their own—they need to be prompted into action. *The Referral Code* shows you how to turn your relationships into referrals easily, effectively, and gracefully. This smart and empowering book should be required reading for anyone who wants to grow their client or customer base."

— Paul David Walker, author of
Unleashing Genius: Leading Yourself, Teams and Corporations

"I need to raise nearly $6 million from film investors, no easy task in this economy! After reading and applying *The Referral Code*, I now have personal introductions to ten potential investors worth over $100 million each."

— Rodney Vance, Hollywood producer and screenwriter

"As an admittedly 'non-salesy' type, I have found it extremely difficult to ask for referrals in the past. *The Referral Code* gives me the keys to reach out for referrals effectively and comfortably, like the best salespeople in the business. The best thing is that this system really works. The big plus is that I don't have to be anyone other than who I am!"

— Tony Rose, CPA and author of *Say Hello to the Elephants*

"Referrals are one of the best ways I know to attract new clients and customers. The Referral Code lays out an ingenious system for motivating the people you know to connect you with future business. Highly recommended!"

— Philip Tirone, author of *Seven Steps to a 720 Credit Score*

Larry Pinci and Phil Glosserman

sell the feeling2 the referral code

Unlock a Constant Stream of Business Through the Power of Your Relationships

NEW YORK

the referral code
by Larry Pinci and Phil Glosserman

ISBN 978-160037-747-1 (paperback)

Library of Congress: 2009943813

Published by:

MORGAN JAMES PUBLISHING
1225 Franklin Ave. Ste 325
Garden City, NY 11530-1693
Toll Free 800-485-4943
www.MorganJamesPublishing.com

Cover Design by:
Rachel Lopez
rachel@r2cdesign.com

Interior Design by:
Bonnie Bushman
bbushman@bresnan.net

In an effort to support local communities, raise awareness and funds, Morgan James Publishing donates one percent of all book sales for the life of each book to Habitat for Humanity.
Get involved today, visit
www.HelpHabitatForHumanity.org.

We dedicate this book to you, our readers. We salute you for creating relationships with people who 'get' who you are and what you bring. We acknowledge you for the steps you have already taken to grow your business and for the new efforts you are about to launch. We know that your relationships will bring you far more than you ever imagined.

"Personal relationships are the fertile soil from which all advancement... all success... all achievement in real life grows."

— Ben Stein

"Every person is a new door to a different world."

— from the movie "Six Degrees of Separation"

"Il n'est qu'un luxe véritable, et c'est celui des relations humaines."

(There is only one true value, and it is human relationships.)

— Antoine de St-Exupéry in Terre Des Hommes

"It's All About Who You Know – and Who They Know"

— Headline from article in Washington Post by Ted Knutson

table of contents

the referral code

get your free bonuses now!

as an appreciation for reading *The Referral Code*, we offer four complimentary bonus reports, a $59 value.

- **The Referral Conversation Quick Reference** – This condensed summary of the referral conversation is an essential companion to the book. Be sure to review it before your ask anyone for referrals.

- **The Referral Matrix Worksheet** – This worksheet is an invaluable aid in setting up and managing your referral game. It will help you come up with potential referral partners and keep track of all your referral conversations. The Referral Matrix is the master document for planning and executing your referral strategy.

- **What Every Business Person Needs to Know about Making and Maintaining Agreements** – A system that will eliminate communication breakdowns in all your negotiations and sales conversations.

To receive your free bonus reports, go to:
www.ReferralCodeBonus.info

preface

for many people, receiving a referral is like getting an unexpected check in the mail—it is a nice bonus and you wish you would receive more of them more often.

The Referral Code is going to take the wishing out of the equation. We are about to show you exactly how to get more qualified business referrals, by design. And once you understand the process, you will see that the Referral Code is about much more than receiving an occasional nice bonus—it is a powerful, ongoing strategy for expanding your business.

That you're reading this says that you are looking for an edge in developing new business. What you might not know is that you already have one: **your relationships**, business and otherwise. Your relationships are one of your most important and valuable assets. They carry the seeds of future business. The people you know can and will bring you referrals when you follow the system described in this book.

The Referral Code is for any professional in any industry who wants to grow his or her business. Regardless of what you call yourself—salesperson, business owner, advisor, consultant, or the like—you can successfully employ the strategies in this book to generate more referrals and grow your business.

Ignore the Referral Code system at your own risk. If you are not consistently tapping into your relationships for referrals, you are neglecting the most powerful source of potential business leads, and you are surely missing out on opportunities.

If you already receive some referrals here and there, we will show you how to tweak your game so you will receive even more. If you have tried or hoped for referrals in the past but have experienced less-than-stellar results, we will show you what has been missing in your game and what you need to do differently to dramatically improve your results.

What is the Referral Code?

The Referral Code is a highly effective system for receiving a constant stream of qualified referrals, now and throughout the entire life of your business. We believe it is the most effective warm-lead-generating system on the planet.

Your relationships—the people you know—have their own networks of relationships, all of which represent a vast treasure chest of potential business for you. The challenge is how to get your relationships to open the chest and personally connect you with the people they know who need what you offer.

The Referral Code is your key to unlocking that treasure. It addresses exactly who, when, how, and how often to ask for referrals. It focuses on the real motivations that will drive people to refer you. It shows you not only how to get referrals, but how to turn them into personalized warm introductions that pave the way for you to create new business. The Referral Code also provides the way to manage your referral-building activities in the midst of your already busy life. And finally, it shows you how to have your relationships continue to bring you more and more referrals over time.

Our approach to referrals is different than any you may have encountered. It is a specific methodology that is strategic, direct, and proactive.

Most of the other referral systems we have seen focus on developing your professional presence through networking, newsletters, and other activities designed to put you and your business in front of people. These activities are designed to help you build mindshare, new relationships, and referrals over time.

The Referral Code takes a more direct approach. Though it is important to cultivate more relationships and build mindshare over time, our system shows you how to start receiving referrals right away.

Most importantly, the Referral Code system works. We have taught it to hundreds of our coaching and sales training clients, and many now use the Referral Code as their primary means of developing new business. Using the same strategies you are about to learn, many of our clients have grown their business by well over 50 percent in 12 months.

We are going to show you how to recruit people you know to become, in effect, your sales force. Imagine your clients, customers, associates, and even friends and family working on your behalf to bring you qualified referrals to people they know who need what you offer. When you follow our system, not only will they bring you referrals, but they will do so happily and willingly. What's more, the people they refer to you will be *qualified* leads who are ready to talk with you.

Warm Beats Cold Every Time!

Now, more than ever, referrals are the best way to create new business opportunities. In today's overcrowded marketplace, you might find tens, hundreds, or even thousands of businesses that offer the same services or products as you. People are inundated with marketing messages, sales pitches, and cold calls. Buyers are becoming more wary and discriminating. As a result, many sellers are finding that the traditional methods of acquiring business leads, such as cold calling, are becoming less and less effective.

We have a saying: *Warm beats cold every time.* Referrals help buyers cut through the clutter. People would much rather do business with a professional or company recommended by someone they know and trust than shop in the open market and run the risk of doing business with someone with whom they have no connection. And as a seller or service provider, you have a much greater chance of connecting and paving the way to do business with a warm referral than you do with a cold lead.

The Importance of Your Relationships

Professionals frequently talk about the importance of relationships in business. *Business runs on relationships and depends on relationships.* Relationships open doors and pave the way to make things happen. Relationships help ensure trust, reliability, competence, and confidence.

We assume you have a number of strong relationships—business and otherwise—and we hope you value and nurture them. The people you know have relationships with people who need to know you. By the time you finish this book, you will know exactly what it takes to have the people in your life connect you with people and organizations that need your services, your products, and you.

Everyone Wins!

Some people reading this may be concerned or even put off by the idea of intentionally generating referrals through relationships. Let's lay that concern to rest right now. This book is not about exploiting your relationships or selfishly using people to further your personal objectives. Instead, it is about creating positive opportunities—not just for you, but for your clients, business associates, friends, and the people they know and care about.

Who better to refer you than the people that already know and respect you, right? It seems like a no-brainer, but for many people, asking for referrals is a struggle or even a no-no. We are going to show you how to make it a yes-yes. If you have limiting beliefs or any hesitation to tap into your relationships for referrals, we will show you how to eliminate your resistance so you can expand your field of opportunities and your business.

The Referral Code system is about everyone winning. That includes you, the people who refer you, and the people they refer you to. Once you understand the **real** reasons people make referrals and learn how to create these win-win-win opportunities, you will be ready to take your referral game to a whole new level.

A System for All Seasons

At the time of this writing (2009), the world economy is in a state of recession. Most professionals and companies have seen a significant decrease in business. Many feel desperate and are scrambling to find new sources of business.

During down cycles, many people become discouraged and let up or give up in their business-development efforts. If you are reading this during a down cycle, we encourage you to charge forward with the Referral Code.

In spite of the current down markets and troubled economic times, our clients have continued to grow their business using the methods described in this book. The Referral Code is one of the best ways to increase your pipeline of opportunities in **any** market. The work you put in now will pay off, and when conditions improve, you will be that much further ahead in your business development.

In *The Referral Code*, we say a lot about managing your business-development activities and your mindset through tough times. Hopefully the outlook for business will have improved by the time you read this. Nevertheless, down cycles in the overall economy or in your particular industry are inevitable. Some of the lessons in this book are designed to support you through those tough times.

The Referral Code system is designed for all seasons—up, down, and in-between. Regardless of the current set of conditions, we encourage you to press through, ignore the naysayers, and continually work the system. You will get out of it what you put into it.

The Big Blockers

Most professionals would love to get more referrals. Yet when it comes to this important and potentially powerful source of new business, many play the referral game circumstantially or even passively.

Most people would agree with the old adage, "Ask and you will receive." Yet when it comes to referrals, most professionals do not ask. And in our experience, of those professionals who do ask, many do so inconsistently, ineffectively, or haphazardly.

We recently surveyed a group of professionals in various industries to learn about their approach to referral business. 97 percent of the respondents said they would like at least half of their business to come from referrals, but more than 80 percent expressed a strong aversion to asking. The responses to one of our survey questions were particularly revealing about the fears and beliefs that hold people back.

"When you think about proactively asking your clients/customers for referrals, do you have any hesitation, and if so, why are you reluctant to ask?"

Here are some of the responses:

"I don't want to be pushy."	"Afraid of sounding desperate or hungry."
"I'm afraid I'm going to put them out."	"Worried that clients/customers will feel 'used' or inconvenienced."
"Always felt like it was asking for a handout, begging, etc."	"I feel like I am imposing."
"Afraid of rejection."	"It makes me feel needy and greedy."

As you will learn, there are three main blockers that stop professionals from asking for referrals:

- They don't know **when** to ask.
- They don't know **how** to ask.
- They're **afraid** to ask.

By the time you are done with this book, not only will you know why it is so important to ask for referrals, but you will also know exactly who, when, and how to ask. We will also dispel any concerns or fears you may have about asking.

A Word About *Sell the Feeling*

The Referral Code is Part II of our *Sell the Feeling* book series. Part I is called *Sell the Feeling: The 6-Step System that Drives People to Do Business with You.*

If you have not read *Sell the Feeling*, do not be concerned. *The Referral Code* builds on the principles we established in *Sell the Feeling*, but it is also designed to stand on its own. In *The Referral Code,* we make numerous references to *Sell the Feeling* and tell you how to download more information if you want it.

Sell the Feeling is based on the principle that people buy based on feelings and decide whether to do business with someone based on feelings.

Similarly, **people refer based on feelings.** In *The Referral Code,* we show you how to maximize the goodwill and good feelings you have already created with people you know so that they will refer you to the people they know.

In short, *The Referral Code* shows you how to receive more referrals so you can land more prospects. *Sell the Feeling* tells you what to do once you get in front of prospects, so you can motivate them to do business with you.

Of course, we encourage you to read *Sell the Feeling*, but as we said, it is not a prerequisite to reading and implementing the referral system we describe in this book.

And Now, a Word from Our Sponsors

Our training and coaching programs take a more intensive and in-depth approach to generating referrals and selling in specific situations and industries. For information on our training, coaching, and audio programs, and other goodies, go to **www.sellthefeeling.com**

Free Bonus!

As our way of saying thanks for buying *The Referral Code,* you are entitled to a free bonus valued at $59. For details, see the bonus page at the beginning of this book.

Okay, let's get down to business. Fasten your seatbelt and get ready to take a ride with some new (and old) friends.

feet to the fire

Click, click, click, click, CLICK, CLICK. Debby instantly recognized the sound of Jennifer's heels echoing down the hallway as she approached her office from the conference room. Her footsteps were brisk and pounding. Debby knew that could mean only one thing: Jennifer was fit to be tied—again.

"Hold all my calls, Debby," Jennifer barked as she slammed her office door shut. Catching herself, Jennifer opened the door, forced a smile, and added, "please," then closed the door again.

Debby had become all-too-familiar with Jennifer's outbursts. They began a month earlier, when the company, in the midst of a major reorganization, brought on a new executive VP of sales.

Inside her office, Jennifer closed her eyes, clenched her fists, and swallowed the expletive she felt like screaming.

The last 18 months had been nearly picture-perfect. She had met and married the man of her dreams, moved into a beautiful townhouse, and taken a promising new job as a senior account executive at PITS, short for Pacific Information Technology Solutions. She loved her job at PITS, that is, until a month ago, when she met Roger Needleman, the new head of Sales. Since then, Jennifer's attitude had spiraled downward. In private moments she had started referring to the company as 'the pits.'

Jennifer was an accomplished salesperson with nine years' experience in high tech. She was smart, great with people, and had a salty edge that often caused her to be dubbed as one of the boys. Jennifer was a closer. When she met with a prospect, chances were good that she'd leave with a sale under her belt.

1

the referral code

Jennifer never had to work to find prospects. Her previous two companies provided her with qualified leads; Jennifer simply reeled in the catch. When PITS recruited Jennifer a year ago, she inherited 16 accounts, most of which were in the mortgage industry. In exchange for a very comfortable livelihood, all she had to do was service, renew, and up-sell her existing accounts, and land new service agreements with their subsidiaries. Piece of cake!

Then the mortgage industry took a nosedive. Five of her accounts were acquired by larger companies, who quickly cut back on expenses by bringing their IT services in-house. Two other accounts went out of business. Four of her clients downsized and cut back on services. For the first time in her career, Jennifer's pipeline was draining.

Needless to say, PITS sales were down—way down. The company was in trouble, and rumors of impending cutbacks and layoffs circulated daily. In an attempt to turn things around, the board of directors shuffled the deckchairs in the executive suite. They recruited Roger Needleman, a tough, authoritarian, old-school sales exec from the industrial maintenance industry, of all places. Roger was from Texas and had spent the last fifteen years driving a sales force to cold call their way into manufacturers and sell them service contracts for industrial equipment.

Jennifer had a bad feeling about Roger when she read his bio in the companywide email announcing his appointment as executive vice president of sales. The manufacturing and high-tech industries were worlds apart. The bio referred to Roger as 'hard-driving.' Jennifer thought, *I have plenty of drive myself, thank you—I don't need some Texan industrial equipment jockey telling me how to run my show!*

Her worst fears were confirmed in a meeting when Roger was introduced to the company. He gave a tough-talking speech, warning employees not to get too comfortable, and to get ready for change. He promised to 'hold the sales department's feet to the fire.' *What a way to inspire the troops,* Jennifer thought.

The troops didn't like it either. In secret bitch-sessions behind closed doors, they gossiped and speculated about how 'Old Needlenose' might hold their feet to the fire. They talked of updating their résumés and jumping ship, if only the economy were in better shape.

Jennifer sat in her office silently recounting today's sales meeting. Roger had rolled out his strategic plan to save PITS. He talked and talked and put all kinds of numbers and graphs on the whiteboard. At the end of the day, Roger's grand plan could be summarized in two words: cold calling. He expected every sales rep to make 75 cold calls a week and turn in weekly call sheets.

Until now, enforced cold calling was not a part of the company's culture. Judging from the looks in the room, no one was happy with the new plan.

Roger bellowed out, "I'm a big believer in accountability. The numbers never lie. We'll soon separate the performers from the non-performers. Tough times call for tough measures. Those who aren't with the program may not be around for the company Christmas party, heh-heh-heh."

Jennifer cringed when she heard Roger's signature sarcastic chuckle. He used it whenever he wanted to 'inspire' someone into action through fear. The chuckle would soon come to grate on Jennifer's nerves like nails on a blackboard.

Back in her office, Jennifer took a couple deep breaths and considered her options. She knew that Roger's cold-calling regime was doomed to fail and that she would never comply with it. She could call a headhunter, but then she would feel like a quitter.

She looked up at her bookshelf and noticed the book, *Sell the Feeling*. It reminded her of what she did best: connect with people, discover their needs, and help them get what they want.

What should she do? What **could** she do? It was clear that she wouldn't buy into Needlenose's demands, but she wasn't about to give up on the position she had carved for herself at PITS. Even though she had been there for only a year, she was considered one of the company's 'rock stars.' It would take a lot more than a down market and some hee-haw sales executive to ruffle her feathers. Jennifer was a 'possibility thinker.' Maybe she could create some alternative arrangement with Needlenose.

the referral code

She decided to call her husband to see if he could offer her any advice. He too was in sales and would probably have some ideas. She called Neil's cell phone, which went to voicemail.

Strange, she thought. He almost always picked up when she called.

Before she could leave a message, her office phone rang. It was her assistant.

Annoyed, Jennifer answered, "Debby, I thought I told you I didn't want to be disturbed."

"I'm sorry, Jennifer, but Mr. Needleman just called. He wants to see you in his office right away."

Jennifer sighed and rolled her eyes. *I wonder what this is about,* she thought. *Maybe he wants to hold my feet to the fire.*

Chapter 2

a celebration cut short

*g*reat job. Way to sell the feeling! Neil congratulated himself as he slipped into his car after another successful sales meeting. He had just bagged a 'big fish.' The CEO of a biotech company had signed on to have Neil manage his personal investment portfolio, valued north of 20 million dollars. Neil couldn't wait to call Jennifer and tell her the good news.

What a great run, Neil thought. Over the past year and a half, he had met and married a fantastic woman, moved into a beautiful home, and grown his business beyond his wildest dreams.

Neil was a changed man. No longer the cynical wannabe despairing over his latest sales slump, he had changed his approach to selling and his entire mental game. And it all started with a clumsy sales pitch he had delivered to an old man who turned out to be the greatest mentor he could ever have hoped to meet: Sam Martin.

Sam was the catalyst that turned Neil's business—and his life—around. When Neil landed on Sam's doorstep with his slick sales presentation two years earlier, Sam threw him out on his ear.

"You're selling the wrong thing," Sam told Neil, who scratched his head in confusion.

Partially out of ego, partially out of desperation, and partially out of curiosity, Neil continued to call on Sam. Eventually, Sam offered to help Neil discover what was missing from his approach to selling. Neil accepted the offer, and over the next year, Sam taught Neil all about selling the feeling.

During their first coaching session, Sam told Neil that people buy based on feelings.

5

"To create sustained business success," Sam said, "you've got to sell the **feelings** that motivate people to want what you're selling and do business with you."

Sam's sales process made a big difference in Neil's game. Neil began to communicate with his buyers in the language of their thoughts and feelings, rather than his own. As he began to relate to people better, his confidence and his closing ratio skyrocketed. Within nine short months, he surpassed 31 salespeople in his company to claim the number-one spot.

Sam also worked with Neil on his mentality. He taught him to be *at-cause*— in charge of his own thoughts, beliefs, attitudes, and actions.

The positive changes Neil made in his business spilled into his personal life. What he learned from Sam about connecting and communicating with people made a big difference when he met and wooed Jennifer.

Neil felt a tremendous sense of gratitude for Sam. He was still amazed that their chance encounter had led to such profound changes in his business and life. It felt like fate.

As Neil basked in the glow of today's sales victory and his ongoing happiness and good fortune, he turned up his CD player and began singing. Little did he know that his fate was about to change again.

At the corner of Main and Fifth, a blue van ran a light and came careening into the intersection, just as Neil was making a left turn. The van slammed into Neil's right front fender and sent his car spinning into the opposing lane. Neil's airbag inflated.

A moment later, another car crashed head-on into Neil.

Within minutes, the police and paramedics were on the scene. Unconscious and caught in a tangled mass of steel, leather, glass, and plastic, Neil did not hear his cell phone ring.

When Neil's phone went to voicemail, Jennifer hung up.

I'll talk to Neil about my problems with Needleman when I get home, she thought.

the pep talk

On her way to Needleman's office, Jennifer ran into Patrick, one of PITS' top salespeople. He looked as if he had just swallowed castor oil.

"You must be next in line for Needleman's pep talk," Patrick said, pursing his lips.

"That bad, huh?"

"You'd think Needleman would want to build bridges with the sales team—get to know us, ask some questions, get the lay of the land. Nope. Get ready for 'The World According to **Roger**.'"

Patrick's tone became sarcastic, "Did you know that **Roger** developed his grit by working as a roughneck on Texas oil wells and as a Navy drill sergeant? Did you hear that **Roger** developed his sales savvy selling vacuum cleaners door-to-door? And, as you'll soon find out, **Roger** rubs elbows with some mighty impressive people."

"Thanks for the warning, Pat. I'll compare notes with you later."

"Just wait till you see the shrine," Patrick added as Jennifer rounded the corner to Needleman's office.

After a 15-minute wait, Jennifer was ushered into Needleman's office by his executive assistant.

"Sorry to keep you waiting," said Needleman. "My old buddy Senator Graham just called to invite me on a deer-hunting trip. He got to talking about our old Navy days, and as you might imagine, I didn't want to cut a U.S. Senator off."

the referral code

Jennifer tried hard not to roll her eyes. Patrick's warning was spot-on. In the first 10 seconds, Needleman had dropped a name and mentioned his time in the Navy.

"Jennifer, come in, sit down, make yourself comfortable."

As Jennifer took in the surroundings, she drew several negative conclusions about Needleman. As Patrick said, the office was a kind of shrine to Roger's ego.

First, there was the photo gallery—20 or so pictures of Needleman, all testaments to his hardy life and the good company he kept. There were photos of a young Needleman working the oil well and photos of Needleman, hunting, boating, and golfing. Several photos showed Roger rubbing elbows with famous politicians, athletes, and other dignitaries.

Then there was the award center—a bookshelf that housed his trophies, plaques, etc.

And finally, the *pies de resistance*: a buck head mounted on the wall right behind Roger's desk.

"A 16-pointer," Needleman boasted when he noticed Jennifer's look of surprise. "A real beauty, Jennifer. I bagged him two years ago on a hunting trip with my buddy Steve Johnson, the CEO of a little outfit you may have heard of, U.S. Banking Trust."

This guy's a living caricature of himself, Jennifer thought as she mentally catalogued his second name-drop in less than two minutes.

"Jennifer, let's talk about how you fit into my new sales strategy."

How I fit into your sales strategy? Jennifer bit her tongue. *This guy really could use a lesson on rapport. What a pig!*

Jennifer quickly composed herself. "Mr. Needleman…"

"Please, call me Roger."

"Okay, Roger," said Jennifer. Instead of launching into a diatribe against his cold-calling mandate, she decided to ask some pertinent questions. "What exactly do you have in mind?"

"Let me tell you a story, Jennifer..."

Roger used Jennifer's name every time he addressed her, as if that were a good way to gain rapport. To her, it felt contrived and inauthentic.

Roger leaned forward in his chair. "After I got out of the Navy, I took a job selling vacuum cleaners door-to-door."

Jennifer leaned forward, matching Roger's body language. She did her best to pretend to care.

"I had never sold anything before, but I figured it would be easy. After all, I had just spent six years in the Navy. How hard could it be selling vacuum cleaners to housewives? I'd just put on the old Needleman charm."

Jennifer suppressed a laugh.

"Well, Jennifer," Needleman continued, "I quickly found out that sales is **hard work**."

Don't patronize me, Jennifer thought, while nodding her head in contrived agreement.

"After a while, I realized that the more homes I hit, the more I sold. I'm pretty competitive by nature, so I decided to hit more than anyone else. After just four months, I became the number-one salesman in my region. By the end of my first year, I was number one in the state. It wasn't long before I was number one in the company."

Jennifer smiled and thought, *Sounds like you're pretty big on Number One.*

"Eventually, they promoted me to national sales director. I went on to become vice president of sales for Robbins International Paper Supply and later Hanford-Wilson Manufacturing. I took Hanford-Wilson from a five-million-dollar company to 12 million in six short years. What I learned selling vacuum cleaners stuck with me for the rest of my career. Do you know what I learned from selling vacuum cleaners, Jennifer?"

You've obviously learned quite a bit about sucking, Jennifer thought.

"What did you learn, Roger?" she asked, feigning interest.

"Jennifer, I learned that you've got to get out there and talk to as many prospects as possible. Sales is a competition and a numbers game. Salesmen— excuse me—sales**people** eat what they kill, and the hunter who takes the most shots, bags the most bucks."

Needleman gave Jennifer a toothy grin, gestured toward the buck head on his wall, and chuckled, "Heh-heh-heh...pun intended!"

There it was again—the same irritating laugh that Jennifer had noticed in the sales department meeting. She was floored by Roger's outright buffoonery. She didn't know how to respond. No matter—Roger didn't give her an opening.

"What I am saying, Jennifer, is that we have to get a whole lot better at getting in front of people. And there are just three ways to do it: cold calling, cold calling, and cold calling. That's why I am requiring that every rep make at least 75 calls each week. We've got to get a lot more aggressive, especially in this market."

"Roger, you're really changing things up around here. A number of our salespeople have been quite successful using methods other than cold calling."

"That may be so, Jennifer, but they'll kick it up a notch once they get onboard with the new program. Look, I realize that we may see some resistance at first, but the troops will adapt. We have got to get lean and mean, Jennifer. Be forewarned—some of your friends may not be at this year's Christmas party. Heh-heh-heh..."

There was the dreaded chuckle again. Apparently, Needleman took a perverse pleasure in threatening to sack people. Jennifer pictured his wall decorated with heads of her coworkers sprouting antlers.

Roger lowered his voice and looked her in the eye. "Jennifer, I need your help."

"**My** help?"

"Jennifer, from what I understand, you're one of the up-and-coming stars and quite well-respected by the rest of the troops. I need you to be the champion—the poster child—for cold-calling success. People will follow your lead."

Feeling like she had some tentative respect from Roger, Jennifer pressed in a bit. "So Roger, 75 calls a week sounds like a lot of time on the phone. I know we can expect to reach a lot of voicemails, dead-ends, assistants screening calls, and things like that. What kinds of success percentages are you looking for? Can you give me some measurable outcomes you expect, like the number of contacts turned into meetings, number of meetings turned into proposals, and number of proposals converted into sales?"

For the first time, Roger paused. He leaned back in his chair, and peered at Jennifer over the tops of his glasses. "I'm impressed," he said.

A knock at the door interrupted Needleman before he could say anything else. His executive assistant opened the door and stuck her head inside.

"Excuse me for interrupting," she said. "Jennifer, you've got an emergency phone call from a Dr. Pearlman at Northview Hospital."

Chapter 4

cold-calling hell

"a freaking whirlwind."

That's how Jennifer described her time-off when she returned to work three weeks after Neil's accident.

So much had happened so fast that she could barely keep it straight. She felt like her world had been turned upside-down and inside-out.

Neil was in the hospital nine days. His jaw and three ribs were broken, and he had numerous cuts, bruises, abrasions, and a minor case of whiplash. The airbag ruptured several blood vessels in his face, leaving him with two black eyes and puffy purple cheeks. He was not a pretty sight.

Fortunately, Neil would make a full recovery, in time. Meanwhile, his jaw was wired shut, meaning he had to endure several weeks of a liquid diet and a limited ability to talk. He wouldn't be able to return to work for up to three months.

Jennifer bought Neil a small chalkboard so he could communicate.

The first message he wrote was, *Crave burger. Run one thru blender, ok?* Jennifer caught herself laughing for the first time in three weeks.

Jennifer realized that Neil could have been killed. Every day, she thanked her lucky stars that her beloved husband was alive and would recover. But she was stressed and troubled. Taking care of Neil the past three weeks had been draining. She shuttled him to doctor appointments, made sure he drank enough calories, and helped him bathe and dress.

the referral code

Besides all this, Jennifer was sitting on a problem of her own—one that she couldn't share with Neil. Though they had some savings and Neil still had certain revenue coming in, Jennifer was now the major breadwinner—this at a time when her existing business was drying up and her new boss was insisting that she spend several hours a day trying to wrangle new business from people she didn't know.

Jennifer resented Needleman and thought his cold-calling plan was a waste of time and beneath her. Under normal circumstances, she would be out looking for a new position. But with Neil out of commission, she felt obligated to tough it out. She decided to keep it all bottled up inside and not burden him with her problems.

When she arrived back at the office three weeks after the accident, she found a beautiful vase of flowers on her desk. The card read,

```
Jennifer,

Welcome back. I wish your husband a speedy recovery. The
team missed you. Feel free to take a day or two to take care
of any loose ends before you hit the phones. When life gives
you lemons, make lemonade!

All the best,
Roger
```

Jennifer cringed. *Make lemonade? What gall! I'd like to tell him to shove those lemons where the sun doesn't shine!*

Only five minutes back in the office and she was already seething.

By two o'clock that afternoon, she had answered her emails and returned her calls. She was ready as she would ever be to launch into the mandatory cold-calling regime.

She looked at the call list. Eighty-four pages listed over thirteen hundred companies. Some included contact names; most just listed the corporate headquarters' toll-free numbers. In addition to Jennifer's disdain for cold calling, the lack of specific points of contact posed an additional challenge: who to ask for when the receptionist answered the phone?

cold-calling hell

In Jennifer's business, it was nearly impossible to predict who made the recommendations or decisions about IT service contracts. It could be the CTO, the IT director, the CFO, the COO, or a purchasing agent. In Jennifer's mind, cold calling was a wild goose chase, at best. Not having a point of contact was like chasing a wild goose while blindfolded.

Jennifer liked to do things systematically. She started by preparing for the day's calls. She researched 20 companies on the Web, looking for the most likely contact.

When she was done with her research, she started making calls. She quickly discovered that when she did not ask for a specific person, she was easily tagged as a cold caller and summarily dispensed.

After a few of those blow-offs, she cooked up a strategy. If she was unsure of for the point of contact, she would tell the receptionist she was conducting an information technology survey and ask who was in charge IT so she could mail out the survey. She would call back the next day and ask for the appropriate person by name. In some cases, she was able to advance beyond the receptionist to the IT person's gatekeeper. More times than not, the gatekeeper brushed her off.

At the end of the week, she identified five patterns of what she began to refer to as 'cold-calling hell.'

The Cut-off

"Hello, Mr. Graham? This is Jennifer Stewart calling from Pacific IT Solutions. How are you today?"

"What is this regarding?"

"I'm calling today to speak with you about your company's IT service program."

Click.

the referral code

The Information Deflection

"We need to look your program over. Please feel free to mail us any information you have."

The gatekeeper was too professional to add the afterthought: *and we will dispose of it accordingly.*

The Voicemail Black Hole

Jennifer never left a message when forwarded to voicemail on a cold call. She knew that the odds of getting a return call were less than those of winning the lottery.

The Gatekeeper Interference

"Mr. Black is out of town."

"Mr. Jones is in a meeting. May I transfer you to his voice-mail?"

"Ms. Parker is unavailable. May I ask what this is regarding?"

"Please leave your number, and I'll see to it that he gets the message."

"Ms. Saunders is extremely busy for the next two weeks. Can you call back after that?"

Not Interested

"Thanks for calling. We're happy with our current service plan. Please remove us from your call list."

Click.

At the end of two weeks of cold-calling hell, Jennifer perused her call log. It represented a tremendous amount of work, with little forward movement.

Hang Ups	14
Request for Information by Mail	26
Not Interested	18
Left Message with Assistant	34
Left Voicemail	0
Unable to Reach IT Person	40
Dead End (company out of business or wrong #)	17
Appointments Made	1

Well, at least I made one appointment, Jennifer thought as she packed up for the weekend.

The following Tuesday, she drove 40 miles to meet the IT director of a large auto parts distribution company—the one meeting that had resulted from two weeks of cold calling. She was hopeful and excited. The company had over 20 stores and was heavily invested in information technology for inventory, distribution, and cataloging.

She pulled into the parking lot. She was early for the meeting, so she called her office voicemail to check for messages.

"Ms. Stewart, this is Angela, Brad Scranton's assistant. Mr. Scranton was called away on an emergency and will be unable to keep his meeting with you this morning. He apologizes for the inconvenience. His calendar is full for the next two weeks because he needs to wrap things up before his vacation. Once he returns and we have a better idea of his schedule, we will call you back. Thanks for your understanding and patience."

Jennifer pounded the steering wheel with her fists and yelled out, "I have **no** understanding, and I have **run out** of patience!"

She fumed with anger and resentment. Not only was this cold-calling initiative ineffective, but it was also humiliating. She was ready to tell Needleman to shove it, but she felt her hands were tied because of Neil's condition and their financial situation. She could look for another job once Neil was back at work, but for now she felt stuck.

the referral code

Jennifer was tough as nails, but in this moment, her work situation, combined with her pent-up feelings about Neil's brush with death, overcame her. She sat in the parking lot of Olson Brothers Auto Parts corporate headquarters and bawled.

kaw thzam!

When Jennifer walked through the front door, Neil read the news all over her face.

He grabbed his chalkboard. The board was small, so Neil had developed an abbreviated style similar to text-messaging. He and Jennifer shared an inside joke: When Neil wrote messages he often mimicked the style of the Lone Ranger's Indian sidekick, Tonto.

This time he wrote, *Mtg no good?*

Jennifer looked at her husband and rolled her eyes. Without saying a word, she went straight to the liquor cabinet and poured herself a drink. She downed it in two gulps then grabbed Neil's chalkboard.

She rubbed out the word *good* and wrote a few choice words of her own:

Mtg no happen.
Asshole no show
Me had it!

Neil shrugged his shoulders and opened his palms, as if to say, "What's up?"

Jennifer could no longer hold back. She told Neil about everything: Needleman's demands, her negative experiences with cold calling, and the cancelled meeting. For the first time, she told him how upset and scared she was about his accident. By the time she was done, she was weeping.

Neil listened intently. When Jennifer was finished, he wrote on his board: *Y u no tell me b4?*

the referral code

"I didn't want to burden you, Honey. You've got enough to deal with."

Me fine. Pls no hold back

Jennifer walked over to Neil, hugged him, and whispered in his ear, "I love you."

They held each other for some time, and then she sighed, "Honey, what am I going to do?"

Neil wrote, *OK w/me if u quit*

"No! I've worked hard at this job. I won't let this one jerk intimidate me into a career decision. There has to be a way I can turn this whole thing around."

Neil struggled to speak through his wired jaw, "Kaw Thzam."

"What?"

"Kaw Thzam!"

"I still don't understand."

Neil grabbed the chalkboard and wrote, *CALL SAM!!*

After a brief pause, Jennifer sighed and said, "I'll think about it."

a view from 10,000 feet

Sam Martin harnessed himself into the tandem hang glider for his maiden voyage.

Joe the pilot looked over at him and asked, "Ready?"

Sam gave Joe a huge grin and a thumbs-up. They took a few steps forward then vaulted off the edge of the precipice into a grey blanket of morning fog and clouds.

The first thing Sam noticed was how strange it felt to have no ground beneath his feet. Then he noticed the silence, save for the whisper of a gentle breeze. The cool mist kissed his cheeks, and his entire body tingled from the thrill of a new and exhilarating experience. Sam began to laugh uncontrollably as he and Joe soared through the clouds over the highest peak in Maui, the great Haleakala volcano.

Joe glanced at his passenger, "How ya' doin'?"

"Ecstatic!" replied Sam.

As they whisked through the cloudbank, a small blue portal appeared in the distance. In a few short seconds, they sailed through the opening and beheld a most spectacular sight: a black expanse of the volcanic crater below, transitioning into a lush green tropical paradise, and in the distance, an endless expanse of blue ocean and sky.

Sam was overcome by a wave of appreciation and gratitude. Over the past two years, his life had taken a new, unexpected direction. At 68 years old, he now had a renewed sense of purpose and was living a full life. From his vantage point nearly 10,000 feet above the earth, he experienced the magnificence of the world he inhabited and felt the connection of all things. He marveled at how a chance meeting two years ago had led him to this magical moment, and so much more.

It all began with a random sales call that set into motion a chain of events that radically changed his life, and the lives of thousands of others. A little over two years ago, Neil, a financial services specialist, knocked on Sam's door and delivered an awkward and unpersuasive sales presentation. Sam, who knew a thing or two about selling, was put off by Neil's phony-baloney sales shtick and threw him out on his ear.

Neil was in a sales slump. He sensed that Sam saw through him and knew something that he needed to know, so he continued calling on Sam.

Eventually, Sam became Neil's mentor and coach and gave Neil a sales makeover. He taught Neil that people buy based on feelings—feelings about the product or service and the person selling it. The secret of sustained success in selling is to evoke certain feelings, especially trust, confidence, and a feeling of being taken care of.

People buy based on feelings. The secret of sustained success in selling is to evoke certain feelings, especially trust, confidence, and a feeling of being taken care of.

Over the course of several months, Sam taught Neil to sell the feeling. Neil was a good student. Within a few months, Neil not only broke through his slump but also became the top producer in his company.

Sam loved mentoring Neil. The experience was so positive that he decided to come out of retirement, write a book about his sales system, and create seminars to teach it to professionals. Sam's book became a bestseller and his training business took off. He was thrilled. Over the past year, he had delivered over 30 seminars, the latest for a group of insurance professionals at a resort hotel in Maui.

a view from 10,000 feet

Sam loved his new career, teaching, coaching, and mentoring. He also loved new adventures. What better way to celebrate his success than to soar like a bird from the mountains to the beach in this lush tropical paradise.

As he drank in the beauty surrounding him and contemplated his good fortune, Sam realized he wouldn't be here were it not for Neil. He decided to call him right then and there to tell Neil what he was doing and express his appreciation. He pulled out his cell phone and keyed in Neil's number.

Jennifer answered the call. "Hello?"

"Hi, Jennifer. It's Sam Martin. You'll never guess where I'm calling from…"

Jennifer was stunned. "Oh, Sam. I'm so glad you called. Hang on a second. Neil, it's Sam—can you believe it?"

"Jennifer, I'm calling from…"

"Sam, Neil and I were talking just this minute. Well, he actually can't talk, and I have this situation, and less than a minute ago Neil suggested I call you, and before I could even think about it, **you** called me. How weird is **that**?"

Once again, Sam felt the connection of all things. Then he realized what Jennifer had just said.

"Why can't Neil talk? Is something wrong?"

"Oh, Sam, things have been so chaotic for the past few weeks, I haven't had a chance to tell you. Neil was in a huge car accident. He's going to be okay, but he broke his jaw, and it's wired shut. He literally cannot talk."

"Oh no! Are you sure he's going to be alright? How are you?"

"It's been pretty stressful. We're both okay, but I want to talk to you about my work situation."

"I want to see the two of you, and of course, I'll be glad to talk with you about your work," said Sam. "I'll be back in town tomorrow. How about I come over around 7:00? I'll bring dinner."

"That would be great, Sam. Neil will be so happy to see you. Me too."

"Good. Give Neil my best."

"By the way, Sam, where did you say you're calling from?"

dinner and a commitment

When Jennifer answered the doorbell, she was surprised to see a man wearing a white smock with two carts in tow.

"Mrs. Stewart?" he asked.

"Yes. Who are you?"

"I'm Ralph, the caterer. I'm delivering your dinner, courtesy of Mr. Martin."

"This is a pleasant surprise," said Jennifer. "I expected Sam to bring takeout. Please come in."

Ralph wheeled in his carts and set the table with his own tablecloth, dishes, silverware, and one of the most beautiful flower arrangements Jennifer had ever seen.

A few minutes later, Sam showed up. He embraced Jennifer and handed her a bottle of Dom Perignon.

"Jen, so wonderful to see you! You look beautiful, as usual."

On seeing Sam, Jennifer began to cry. He put his arm around her shoulders.

"Sam, so much has happened since we last saw you. Neil was banged up pretty badly. Like I told you on the phone, he's going to be fine, but this whole thing gave me such a scare. And on top of that, they threw me a real curveball at work. I'll tell you about it later."

the referral code

At that moment, Neil walked in. He gave Sam a wiry grin, then held up his chalkboard on which he had written, *Beware the monster!* He lifted his hands, curled his fingers like claws, and made his scariest face.

Sam gave Neil a big hug. "Good to see you. Dear God, what have they done to you?"

Neil scribbled, *Enforced vow of silence. My lady speaks for me.*

Neil noticed the dinner Ralph was laying out and looked at Jennifer.

"I know just what you're thinking," she said to Neil. "Sam always creates a memorable experience."

Neil nodded in agreement and wrote, *Sam always sells the feeling, even when he's not selling!*

Jennifer added, "Sam this is beautiful and so thoughtful. Unfortunately, Neil can't chew. I was so caught up with all that has happened that I forgot to tell you that he's on a liquid diet."

"Not to worry," Ralph interjected from the dining room. "Mr. Martin made me aware of your husband's current restrictions. I have prepared an assortment of gourmet soups and purées for Mr. Stewart, as well as a special key lime custard for dessert."

Jennifer looked at Sam and smiled, "I can't tell you how good it feels to be taken care of right now!"

Neil tapped his chalkboard, which still displayed the message, *Sam always sells the feeling.* Neil and Sam gave each other knowing grins.

Over a delicious dinner, Sam, Jennifer, and Neil caught up. Sam told them about the seminars he had been leading and waxed rapturously about his hang-gliding experience.

After dinner, Neil left Jennifer and Sam alone to discuss her situation. Jennifer told Sam all that had happened at work and described her frustration

26

with Needleman's cold-calling mandate. Sam listened attentively as Jennifer spilled her guts.

When she was done, Jennifer let out a deep breath and asked, "Can you help me with this, Sam?"

Sam smiled. "I'm pretty sure I can, Jen, but before we go after this, I have a question for you. You don't have to answer tonight. You have a choice to make, and I want you to consider it carefully."

"Sure, Sam. What is it?"

"Do you want me to help you get better at cold calling, or do you want to develop a warm lead-generating system which will feed you **qualified leads** way beyond the effort and energy that you directly put into it?"

"I don't have to think about this—I can tell you right now," said Jennifer. "I can't stand cold calling. I can't imagine anything you could teach me that could possibly change that. I'm at the end of my rope. Even though I've been in sales for 10 years, the companies I've worked for have pretty much provided me with all the leads I ever needed. So I'm pretty new at this. If you can show me how to get great new leads, and if they are qualified like you say, I'm all for it!"

"Good—I was hoping you'd say that. At some point, you are going to have to deal with your boss and address the whole cold-calling thing, but we'll cross that bridge when we get to it. I want you to understand that my coaching you requires a commitment on your part. It could take a few weeks or even months for me to coach you through this. It will take time and energy. For the time being, you are going to have to find room for this in your schedule, in addition to the required cold calling and, of course, taking care of Neil."

Jennifer gave Sam a determined look and replied, "I need to improve my situation. I'll do whatever it takes."

Then something occurred to Jennifer. "Sam, obviously this is going to take time on your part. You're a busy man. How can I make it worth **your** while?"

Sam recalled the feeling of gratitude that he experienced while hang gliding. "Jen, it would be my pleasure to work on this with you. My experience coaching

the referral code

Neil brought me more than you can possibly know. Let's just say this will be my way of giving back—you know, paying it forward."

"Giving back? **You** were the one who helped turn Neil's business around!"

Sam lowered his voice. "The circle travels in both directions and never ends."

"You're the best," Jennifer told Sam. "I am so grateful and excited about getting your help with this!" She gave him a big hug.

"You are most welcome. One more thing," Sam continued, "and this is important. I need your absolute commitment that you will attend all of our meetings, do all the assignments, and complete the process. I know we're good friends and that right now you're determined, but you have to have some skin in the game."

"What do you mean?" Jennifer asked.

"Is there a cause or a political party or candidate that you would absolutely hate giving your money to?"

Jennifer laughed. "You **are** sly, Sam. Let me think." A few seconds went by, then Jennifer's eyes lit up.

"You want to know who I'd hate giving my money to? Corky Starr. He's running for state legislature in our district. I went to high school with Corky. He was always running for some student body office or another. He was an egomaniac and the epitome of a slick politician even back then. I didn't like him then, and I don't like him now. I've been reading about his positions on the issues. He stands for everything I detest."

"Great," said Sam. "I'd like you to write a $10,000 check to Corky's campaign and give it to me. I'll only mail him the check if you don't stick to our agreement."

Jennifer shuddered. "That's a great incentive, Sam. But there are a couple of problems. With Neil not working, we really don't have that kind of money sitting around. Besides, I think the maximum legal campaign contribution is $4000.

28

Believe me, it doesn't matter whether the amount is $10,000 or $10—it would make me sick to give Corky Starr any kind of contribution!"

"Okay, then write a $4,000 check to Corky's campaign. If you keep your commitment, I'll tear it up," said Sam.

Jennifer retrieved her checkbook from her purse. Sam noticed the color drain from her face as she wrote the check.

"Here's the check," said Jennifer with a sigh. "When do we begin?"

"I have an assignment for you right now. I want you to contact 10 successful salespeople and find out what methods they use to develop new business leads. Can you do it by next Tuesday?"

"Yes."

"Great. Let's meet Tuesday morning for breakfast at Patty's Diner," said Sam.

After writing down the address, Jennifer said, "I'll be there, Sam. And thank you so much!"

Jennifer didn't tell Sam that she did not personally know 10 successful salespeople. But she was determined to make whatever contacts she needed. When Jennifer put her mind to something, there was no stopping her.

introducing the referral code

Jennifer was unfamiliar with Patty's Diner. As she neared the destination, she wondered if she was in the right place. The streets were lined with warehouses, shipping containers, and industrial buildings.

Sam loves fine food and great impressions. Why the heck is he bringing me all the way out here?

She rounded a corner and saw Patty's Diner sandwiched between a factory and a warehouse. It was 7:30 in the morning; already, there was a line of people outside the door. To Jennifer's surprise, many of them were in business attire.

What's the deal with this place? What's going on here?

Jennifer parked and walked to the front door. Sam was waiting for her.

"Great you found it and right on time. Come on in. Patty is holding a table for us."

The place was packed. As they walked to their table, several of the patrons and waiters greeted Sam by name. As soon as they sat down, an elderly waitress with a beehive hairdo and a pink uniform greeted them with a smile.

"Sam, so good to see you today. You're looking fit as ever."

She turned her attention to Jennifer and smiled warmly. "Hello dear. How are you?"

Sam made the introduction, "Tilley, this is Jennifer. It's her first time here."

"Nice to meet you dear. Would y'all like coffee today?"

the referral code

After Tilley filled their cups and handed them menus, Jennifer asked Sam, "What's the story with this place? I've never seen a diner packed this early in the morning. And it's out in the middle of nowhere. What are all these business people doing in this part of town?"

Sam replied, "When people love something they're willing to let others know, especially the people they love and respect."

Just then, another woman in a pink uniform walked by and Sam flagged her down. "Patty, can you come here for a minute? I'd like you to meet someone.

"Patty, this is my dear friend, Jennifer Stewart. Jennifer, this is Patty O'Flarrety, the owner of this fine dining establishment. This is Jennifer's first time here. She just asked me why you have such a big crowd so early in the morning."

"Nice to meet you, dear," said Patty warmly. "We like to think we have the best breakfast in town, but you want to know the truth? This place is packed because of people like Sam. You see, dear, he brings people here all the time, and he tells all his friends about this place. I have people coming in all the time saying that Sam sent them."

Jennifer was beginning to experience what Neil had told her: everything Sam does has a lesson behind it.

As she read the menu, she noticed an item printed in big letters and surrounded by a box.

> *Sam's Special: 2 pumpkin pecan pancakes, 2 chicken apple fennel sausages, 2 eggs, and freshly squeezed orange juice. Highly recommended!*

Jennifer and Sam both ordered Sam's Special. Then Sam asked, "Did you do your homework?"

"Yes, I did, but it took some doing. You see, Sam, I don't personally know 10 highly successful salespeople."

"How did you reach them?"

"I made some calls, asked around, and people pointed me to other people they knew. It took some networking, but I did manage to talk with 10."

"Good for you! It's amazing what can happen when you tap into the people you know as a resource to connect to others. What did you find out?"

"It's interesting, Sam. I talked to people in different industries, and they all had different things to say about how they build their business, but when you boil it down, there was a common theme. They even used the same word over and over."

"And what word is that?"

"**Relationships**. They said that the people they had the best relationships with referred them business again and again. It makes perfect sense. I guess I've always known intuitively that relationships were important in business, but hearing it from these folks really made it clear to me. I guess I need to focus more on my relationships."

"What do you mean when you say 'focus more on my relationships?'"

Jennifer went blank. After a long pause, she improvised, "In addition to giving my clients great service, I could call them, take them to lunch, and send them articles that would interest them, send them birthday cards, gifts, and email them. I can create a newsletter and send it to them. You know…stuff like that."

"Sounds good to me, Jen. You have time for all that, right?"

Jennifer sighed, "To tell you the truth, Sam, I get exhausted just thinking about these kinds of activities. I suppose I could get my assistant to handle a lot of these things. These days, it takes all the energy I can muster to focus on the work at hand and take care of my husband. I don't even see my friends and family lately. But if that's what I have to do, I'll make myself. I've got to do a better job managing my relationships!"

Sam asked, "For what purpose?"

"So I'll get more referrals."

the referral code

"How is managing your relationships going to get you more referrals?"

Jennifer went blank again.

Sam saved her, "Do you think more phone calls, lunches, gifts, emails, newsletters, and things like that will automatically get people to refer you?"

"Probably…maybe," Jennifer responded with a touch of doubt in her voice.

"Jen, you have your hands full with your work and your relationship at home, not to mention your friends and family. Do you really see yourself hammering out a newsletter, doing lots of lunches, and sending out cards on a regular basis?"

"Honestly, it doesn't sound like something I would do consistently, Sam."

"Jen, all these so-called relationship-building activities are fine. Some people use them quite effectively. I call them 'professional presencing activities' because the objective is for you to establish a greater presence in the minds of those who can help grow your business. Professional presencing might help bring you some referrals over time. It might cause some people to think of you when a referral opportunity arises, or they may feel a sense of obligation. But in my experience, presencing, in and of itself, is not enough to get most people to refer you."

Jennifer was impatient. "Okay, let's get to it. What's the alternative—what do I do instead?"

"We'll get there, Jen. We have a lot of ground to cover. First, let's get clear about this whole notion of business relationships. The term 'relationships' is fuzzy. It has become a buzzword. People use it in different ways to mean different things. I'll tell you what it means to me. A relationship is an emotional connection between people. The emotion could be love, respect, a feeling of relatedness, a common bond over personal or business history, or just plain liking each other."

A relationship is an emotional connection between people.

Sam continued, "Relationships are key. Business runs on relationships. Business depends on relationships.

"As you know, most people in business are extremely busy. Some have trouble finding

34

enough time for their important personal relationships, let alone managing business relationships.

"You said that you need to focus more on your relationships, as if you need to put more time into them. That's not necessarily true. Business relationships are more about quality than quantity. Business relationships should not be judged by the amount of time you spend, but rather the **goodwill** you create in the time you do spend."

Business runs on relationships. Business depends on relationships.

➡

"What exactly do you mean by goodwill?" Jennifer asked.

Sam continued, "Goodwill is a feeling of appreciation developed as a result of taking good care of someone's business needs, or even their needs outside of business. You've created goodwill with your clients, haven't you?"

"I'm sure I have," said Jennifer. "But who really knows? Goodwill is such an intangible thing."

"Goodwill may seem intangible, but believe me, it is **real** and it has power—that is, if you know how to use it. Goodwill is the emotional currency of business relationships."

"I like that," said Jennifer enthusiastically. "So besides taking good care of my clients' needs, is there any other way to develop goodwill?"

"Yes!" Sam exclaimed as he slapped his hand on the table. Jennifer noticed several people turn their heads when Sam hit the table.

Goodwill is the emotional currency of business relationships.

➡

"You sell the feeling, over and over, with every interaction and communication," said Sam. And when you sell the feeling, you evoke trust, confidence, and a feeling of being taken care of. That's what creates and sustains relationships. You read *Sell the Feeling*, didn't you? It probably wouldn't hurt to read it again."

"I did, and I will," Jennifer replied. "So are you saying that people should refer me to repay me for the goodwill I've created? If that's the case, where are the referrals?"

"Good question. Before I answer it, let me ask you a question: Why **should** someone refer you?"

Jennifer thought for a moment and replied, "Because I go out of my way to do a good job for people. I treat them well and create value for them. Hopefully, they'll realize it and send me business in return."

Sam chuckled, "**Hopefully?** Hopefully, I'll win the lottery."

Sam deepened his voice and accentuated his southern drawl, "Hopin', wishin', wishin', hopin.' All that leads to is waitin' and more waitin'. Kind of passive, don't you think?"

Jennifer felt her blood begin to boil. She had never been irritated with Sam before, but had just hit a nerve.

Me, passive? Who does he think he's talking to?

Jennifer had no tolerance for passivity. She saw herself as a go-getter—a woman of action. Sam had intentionally pushed her buttons. He instinctively knew the way to get Jennifer's attention was to challenge her.

Using his sensory awareness, Sam saw the color change in her face and noticed that she was clenching her teeth.

Jennifer shot back defensively, "Honestly, Sam—if I were **passive** would I be sitting here with you?"

Sam just stared back.

"Okay, I give up," she said haughtily. "Why **should** people refer me?"

Sam softened his voice, "Great question, and it deserves a great answer. I want you to think about it for a while. We'll get to it another day."

Neil had warned Jennifer that Sam sometimes dangled tidbits without giving you the full morsel until he thought the time was right. It was his way of keeping you on your toes and getting you to think.

Jennifer asked, "What does all this goodwill have to do with getting referrals?"

"Everything," said Sam. "Your relationships carry the seeds of future business. I'm going to show you how to leverage the goodwill that you've already created with your clients, associates, friends, and even your family, so that they give you more business referrals than ever before. And if you work this system steadily, over time, you will never have to make another cold call again—unless, of course, you want to."

Jennifer's anger subsided and she lit up, "Sounds great!"

Sam continued, "When you think of goodwill, who comes to mind? Who is someone in business that has created massive goodwill with you?"

Your relationships carry the seeds of future business.

➤

Jennifer answered right away, "Joe Benson, the contractor who remodeled our kitchen."

Sam asked, "How did Joe create goodwill?"

Jennifer replied, "He did a great job and was a pleasure to work with. He always did exactly what he said he was going to do, his communication and follow-up were impeccable, plus we could tell he cared, not just about the work, but about us as people. Joe definitely sells the feeling."

"So you love Joe's work and the experience of working with him?"

"Definitely."

"Would you refer Joe to your family, friends, and associates?"

"Absolutely!"

"Have you referred him?"

"Not yet, but I certainly would if the need came up."

"Good. Right now, is there anyone you could refer him to—someone who may be building a house or planning a remodel anytime in the future? Think about it."

Jennifer paused for a moment then responded, "Actually, one of my coworkers wants to add a room to his house next year. And come to think of it, last week I saw a contractor's truck sitting outside our neighbor's house. She later told me she's getting bids for a remodel."

"So did you tell them about Joe?"

"No, I just didn't think about it. I've got so much else on my mind."

"So Joe could have a shot at that business, and you would have referred him, but you didn't think about it, even though you love him and his work?"

Jennifer sighed, "I feel bad. I'll call them both. I hope it's not too late. I just didn't make the connection—I wasn't thinking about it."

"Exactly—you weren't thinking about it. Just like most people. Only about five percent of people are natural promoters—you know, the kind of people who are consistently motivated to refer, connect, and put people together. For example, I'm a natural promoter. When I find something I really like, I tell all my friends. It's just something I do naturally. It's what I did when I discovered Patty's Diner."

Only five percent of people are natural promoters. The other 95 percent have to be suggested into action.

Sam continued, "But not everyone is like me. Remember, only five percent of people are natural promoters. The other 95 percent have to be suggested into action. The point is, that if you want to maximize your opportunity for receiving referrals, you've got to *ask*. My guess is that Joe never asked you."

"No, he didn't."

"If he had asked, would you have recommended him?"

introducing the referral code

"Of course."

"Okay, you get the point. One more thing: there are different ways to ask, and the way most people ask is like batting in the wind."

"Okay, I'm game. How do I ask?"

"That will have to wait until another day."

Damn—there he goes again! Jennifer caught herself wanting to jump ahead. She realized she needed to let Sam unfold the lessons at his own pace.

Sam sensed Jennifer's impatience. "Jen, I appreciate that you're eager to learn and move forward. I promise that I'll get to all your questions in good time. I'm going to teach you to master the most powerful warm lead-generating system I've ever encountered. I call it **the Referral Code**. It will give you the way to tap into your relationships and unlock a constant stream of qualified referrals, now and throughout the entire life of your business.

The Referral Code is the way to tap into your relationships and unlock a constant stream of qualified referrals, now and throughout the entire life of your business.

"By the time we're done, you will know what it takes to get more referrals. You will know exactly who, when, how, and how often to ask. You will know how to motivate people to refer you, not just once, but again and again. The beauty of it is you're going to have your clients do some of the work for you—they're going to give you qualified business leads and warm them up for you. You'll be able to use this system for the rest of your career. It will take a bit of time and effort to set up your game, but believe me, it will be worth it."

"I'm excited, Sam." Realizing that in her impatience she may have come off as ungrateful, she added, "And I really appreciate that you're willing to help me."

the referral code

"It's my pleasure, Jen. By now, I'm sure you've gathered that this isn't about sitting back and waiting for referrals to magically appear just because you're so wonderful and deserving. You're going to have to be proactive, and it's going to take some work on the front end. Speaking of which, I have some homework for you."

Jennifer got out her notebook and a pen.

Sam continued, "I want you to go through your client list and figure out how many clients you have and what percentage of them referred you business over the past year, even if it didn't pan out."

*Your **referral type** is the criteria of the people or companies you're looking to be referred to. It could be type or size of company, number of employees, or a number of other criteria. It could be the position, occupation, or situation of the individuals you want to meet.*

"Okay, I can do that."

"Once you've determined the percentage of clients who referred you, decide what you'd like that percentage to be over the next 12 months.

"I also want you to determine your **referral type**—in other words, the criteria of the people or companies you're looking to be referred to. It could be type or size of company, number of employees, or a number of other criteria. It could be the position, occupation, or situation of the individuals you want to meet. You can look at your client list and figure out what your clients have in common, then decide what criteria best characterize the kind of referrals that you want. This is critical—you've got to get all this done before we can move forward. Let's meet next week. How about Tuesday evening? We'll need a few hours. I'll pick you up at 5:30."

"Works for me. Where are we going?"

Ever the mystery man, Sam replied, "Someplace fun. Be sure to bring your homework."

Jennifer wasn't big on surprises. She liked to know where she was headed at all times. She knew by now not to press Sam for more information, so she held her tongue.

Ugh—I don't like being led by the nose like this! She reminded herself to be patient. *I've got to play by his rules. He's doing me a big favor.*

Just then, Patty came by the table.

"Everything alright? How was your first visit to Patty's, Jennifer?"

"Great food, great service. Thanks, Patty."

"I'm delighted that you enjoyed it, my dear. I look forward to seeing you next time. Here's a coupon for a free breakfast for you and a friend."

"Thanks so much Patty. I'll be back."

As they made their way to the door, Jennifer asked Sam, "Patty's a natural promoter, right?"

"Yes. Did you notice what she did? Besides giving you the coupon, she laced the conversation with suggestions for you to become a future customer. She talked about your first visit to Patty's, as if there would be more, and then said she was looking forward to seeing you next time. And you bought into her suggestions. You said you'd be back. It all seemed very natural didn't it?"

"Yes, it did, Sam."

As Sam walked Jennifer to her car he added, "Suggestions are a wonderful thing when you know how to use them."

As they said good-bye, he added, "By the way, great job at getting referrals to 10 successful salespeople. I predict you'll do great with the Referral Code—that is, once you grasp the nature of the game."

As Jennifer drove off, she thought, *Nature of the game—what the heck is he talking about? I wish he would just cut to the chase!*

Chapter 9

the nature of the game

Sam picked Jennifer up at 5:30 on Tuesday. It was a beautiful fall afternoon, and he had the top down on his baby blue convertible sports car—the one he had received as a gift from a devoted student. Sam was all smiles. Jennifer wondered what he had in store for her today.

"What's all the mystery about, Sam? Where are you taking me?"

Sam asked, "Are you a baseball fan?"

"Not really, Sam."

The truth was, Jennifer thought baseball was boring. She viewed spectator sports as the 'ultimate passive couch-potato non-activity.' She had learned to tolerate Neil's watching sports on TV by going out for a run or reading in another room.

"We're headed over to the Clubhouse Sports Bar to watch the National League playoffs," said Sam, "Even if you're not a fan, you can learn a lot from the game of baseball."

Jennifer suppressed a groan. The last place she wanted to be was in a sports bar with a bunch of drunken, rowdy baseball fans.

When they arrived at the Clubhouse, Jennifer's worst fears were confirmed. The place was packed and the crowd was lubricated and loud. She felt totally out of place.

"Not your kind of crowd, I take it," Sam said with a twinkle in his eye. "Follow me." He escorted Jennifer up a flight of stairs, then down a hall to a green door. He pulled a key from his pocket, unlocked the door, and led her into a small quiet private bar. There were only six patrons.

The bartender greeted them, "Sam Martin, long time, no see. Welcome. Who is your friend?"

"Hi Stan. This is Jennifer Stewart. Jennifer, meet Stan Fenton. Not only does he make the best margarita in town, but he's also a walking encyclopedia of baseball. Ask him anything."

Despite her indifference toward the game, Jennifer decided to play along.

"Pleased to meet you, Stan." Pulling a sports trivia question out of thin air, she asked, "Okay, who won the 1932 World Series?"

Stan grinned, "The New York Yankees beat the Chicago Cubs four games in a row. It was an interesting series. Over those four games, the Yankee's first baseman, Lou Gehrig, was on fire. He had a 529 average batting average, including three home runs. He scored nine runs and eight RBIs. As I'm sure you know, Babe Ruth did a legendary thing in the third game."

Jennifer replied, "Actually, I don't know anything about it. What happened?"

Jennifer listened with curiosity as Stan told the story.

"The score was tied four to four. The game was in Chicago and the home crowd jeered the Babe when he came up to bat. He raised his hand and pointed to the centerfield wall as if to say, 'I'm going to knock it over that fence.' The next pitch came and that's exactly what he did! The legend is often referred to as 'the called shot.' Some baseball historians dispute whether the Babe actually pointed to centerfield before knocking the ball out of the park, but nevertheless, it's a great story."

"I'm impressed," said Jennifer.

Sam jumped in, "The great baseball coach Tommy Lasorda once said, 'There are three types of players: those who make it happen, those who watch it happen, and those who wonder what happened.'"

the nature of the game

Jennifer chuckled nervously. Internally, she was sizing herself up. What type was she when it came to generating new business?

Sam and Jennifer both ordered one of Stan's margaritas.

"I'm curious, Jen," said Sam. "How did you happen to come up with that question about the 1932 World Series?"

"I don't know anything about baseball, Sam. I just said the first thing that came to me."

Sam stroked his chin, "Interesting. Sometimes the universe provides just the right cue at the right time. That story about Babe Ruth is the perfect metaphor for making it happen. That's what you have to do to win at the referral game. You set your sights and go to bat, ignoring any noise or distractions that might discourage you or cause you to hesitate. You take charge of your own game."

They sat down in a quiet booth. The television above the bar was on, but the volume was turned all the way down. Each booth was wired with speakers and equipped with a volume control so the patrons could adjust the sound at their tables.

"Sam, I do feel more comfortable in this room. At least we can talk. What is this place, and how come you have a key?"

"Stan's dad was a good friend of mine and a die-hard sports fan," said Sam. "He even named his son after the great baseball player, Stan Musial. He opened this bar about 25 years ago. The place became so popular that during major sporting events, you could barely see or hear the TV. He decided to create this private bar as a refuge for himself and his friends. He gave us keys so we could come up here and enjoy the major events together. When he died, he left the place to Stan, who kept up the tradition."

Jennifer said, "It's amazing he remembers all those numbers. He must be some kind of sports geek."

"He is amazing, but I assure you he's no geek. He truly **gets** the game of baseball. In baseball, the numbers are critical.

the referral code

"The same goes for business," continued Sam, "but it's surprising how few professionals pay attention to certain critical numbers. If they did, they might see what's missing in their game. Before you can meaningfully track your numbers, you need to understand the nature of the game. To master the Referral Code, you've got to understand what the game is really about and what makes it work."

At that moment, Stan brought their drinks along with a couple bags of peanuts in the shell.

Peanuts, thought Jennifer. *The best part of baseball.*

"Stan," Sam asked, "We were wondering why you are so infatuated with baseball statistics."

"I love the game and its history," said Stan, eager to talk about his favorite subject. "The numbers tell you almost everything—the teams that are positioned to win and why, their strengths and weaknesses, how to strategize against the opposing team, who to put in the line-up, what players to watch out for. I could go on and on, but the bottom line is the numbers and the game on the field go hand-in-hand. You can't fully understand or appreciate one without the other. People say a lot about baseball and what makes one team or player successful. But in the end, the numbers say it all. The numbers don't lie."

Sam turned to Jennifer, "The same goes for business. I couldn't have said it better."

When Stan returned to the bar, Sam asked Jennifer, "Did you come up with your referral type?"

"Yes, I did. We typically work with small- to medium-size companies with at least two hundred employees." She chuckled and added, "Although, I wouldn't turn down a big whale, if you know what I mean."

The pre-game show was beginning. Sam said, "Let's turn up the sound for just a few minutes, alright?"

For the next 10 minutes, Jennifer humored Sam. She bit her tongue as they watched the commentators discuss the teams, players, statistics, and strategies for the playoffs. She was bored out of her mind. Three-quarters of the way through her margarita, she lost her patience and her inhibitions.

"Sam, I get what you're saying about the importance of numbers and statistics in baseball and how the same goes for business, but honestly, what does all this have to do with me getting referrals?"

Sam answered, "A lot of people think that professional baseball is just a bunch of overgrown kids pitching, hitting, running, and fielding. There's much more to it than meets the eye. The Referral Code is no different. If you want to maximize your referrals, you've got to understand the nature of the game you're playing."

"Okay, like what?"

"Like what outcomes you're after, what game you're actually playing, your strategy for winning, how you control the game, who's on your team and how to motivate them, what plays to use in different situations, how to pace your game, and last but not least, keeping score."

Keep Score

Jennifer was getting irritated with the whole business-sports analogy. "Winning? Keeping score? What are we talking about here? I'm trying to get a few referrals so I can get some more business, not beat someone else for gosh sakes!"

Sam replied, "You may not be trying to beat someone else, but surely you want to measure yourself against some standard or goal. You are in sales, so you should be accustomed to scores, like sales quotas, conversion ratios, and things like that."

Sam called out, "Hey, Stan, can you step over here for a moment."

When Stan came to their table, Sam said, "Tell Jennifer what that baseball coach once said about the nature of the game."

the referral code

Stan recited, "The game of baseball is never about the scores until you truly understand the nature of the game—then it's always about the scores."

The game is never about the scores until you truly understand the nature of the game—then it's always about the scores.

➡

"Stan," said Sam, "Tell Jennifer what the difference is between a 200 and a 300 hitter."

Stan answered, "A 200 hitter gets two hits for every 10 times at bat, and a 300 hitter gets three."

"Thanks, Stan." Stan returned to the bar. Sam turned to Jennifer and asked, "Do you know what those numbers really mean?"

Jennifer shrugged.

Sam told Jennifer, "In the major leagues, that one additional hit in 10 is worth millions of dollars in salary!

"How about the game you're playing? How much is one additional client worth to **you** in terms of your commissions and bonuses over the course of a year?"

Jennifer answered, "Depending on the client or the project, a new account could be worth anywhere between $15,000 and $100,000 in commission to me."

"And if you retain that client for three years, what would that give you?"

"My company emphasizes new client development, so we have a diminishing commission structure for contracts that extend beyond 12 months. It would depend on the project."

Sam replied, "Even though the commission percentage decreases, any client you hold onto still pays out over time. And that doesn't even factor in the potential for referrals that could come from that new client. If, by paying attention to your scores, you could tweak your game to bring in two or three additional clients a year, or maybe even five or six, do you see how that could add up, especially over time?"

"Yes, big-time!"

"Good. Let's check out your scores for the last season. How many referrals did you receive over the past year?"

"Actually, I'm embarrassed to say that I only received three that I can remember. Only one of those panned out."

"Where did they come from and how did you get them?"

"One came from a client, another came from a vendor, and the third one came from someone I met at a party. To tell you the truth Sam, I didn't ask for any of these. They just sort of happened."

"So by cruising along on auto-pilot, you got three referrals, one of which turned into business. Imagine what's going to happen when you learn how to play the game and focus your time and energy on it."

"I'm ready!"

"By the way, Jen, did any of your clients refer you into other divisions of their companies or subsidiaries?"

Jennifer thought for a moment. "Yes. One of my corporate clients acquired another company. The client referred us to the new acquisition, and I got the contract. But that was kind of an automatic thing. Is that really a referral?"

"Absolutely—they referred you in. So that makes four referrals, two of which came from your clients. How many clients do you have?

Jennifer took out her PDA and looked through her client base. "As you know, Sam, there's been some attrition lately, due to the economy. Up until recently I had sixteen clients, but right now I'm down to nine accounts."

Sam responded, "So of the sixteen clients you had over the past year, two gave you referrals. That's a little over twelve percent."

"That's right."

"Dollar-wise, what percentage of your new business last year came from the two referrals that panned out?"

Jennifer did some calculations. "Around 30 percent, I think."

"And the referrals you received last year—you got them all without asking, right?"

"Yes."

"Did you ask any of your clients for referrals?"

"Not that I can remember. I had a pretty full plate of inherited business when I came on-board. All I had to do was keep my clients happy and the business kept flowing. Other than that, my company gave me some leads, but I wouldn't call those referrals."

"So let's look at your numbers. You got 30 percent of your new business from referrals last year, without asking. What do you think will happen once you know how to ask and you actually do ask?"

"I'll probably get a lot more."

"Okay, how many of your clients do you want to ask for referrals over the next 12 months?"

Jennifer took out her PDA and looked through her client base and jotted some names in her notebook. After about a minute she responded, "I think I can ask four of them for referrals."

"Four? Why not more?"

"I'm relying on the ones I have a good feeling about."

"Jen, how come you've chosen not to feel good about the others?"

Sam's question stopped Jennifer in her in her tracks. She muttered, "I'm just trying to be realistic."

"You call your limiting belief about the majority of your clients **realistic**?" Sam cranked up his intensity. "Listen to me. Your mentality is your reality. If you want to play a bigger game, you've got to raise your standards and your expectations. There are hoards of people who never get ahead in business or in life because they want to be, as you say, realistic."

Jennifer let Sam's remark sink in for a moment, then responded, "Point taken, but even if I ask every one of my clients for referrals, I can't expect them all to refer me, can I?"

Sam replied, "What you believe is what you'll receive. The great hockey player Wayne Gretzky once said, 'You miss 100 percent of the shots you don't take.'"

What you believe is what you'll receive.

Jennifer nodded in agreement, and wrote the quote in her notebook.

The *Real* Reason People Refer You

Sam went on, "Let's dig a little deeper into the nature of the game and maybe you'll reconsider what is realistic. Remember last time I asked you why people should refer you?"

Jennifer replied, "Yes, I came up with a few reasons: I think my clients genuinely like me. I provide them with great service. I return their calls right away. I give them all the info and help they need. Also, my company provides excellent systems and great service. The bottom line is that we're the best."

"Don't you think your competitors say many of the same things, especially the part about providing great service? Everyone says that. Jen, those are all features. They're all about you—what you or your company does or provides."

Sam continued, "It's good that you provide great systems and services, but I'm asking you to go beyond what you do. What are the benefits? What do your clients get? What does working with you and your company do for them? How does it save or give them more time, money, or energy? How does it streamline their efficiency or make them more effective or productive? What do they get and how do they feel as a result?"

the referral code

Jennifer responded, "We definitely save them time, money, and energy. We make their lives easier because we take all the information technology stuff off their shoulders, and that means they can focus on what they do best. I think they feel good about the whole experience. Many of them tell me that we make their lives much easier."

"Great—those are some of the benefits of working with you. Let's get back to the original question: Why should your clients refer you? What's in it for them?"

Jennifer thought for a moment and responded, "It's a way to pay me back and say thanks for a job well-done."

"So you think that they feel like they owe you? Jen, that's why they're paying your company, isn't it?"

"Yes."

"Let's take payback out of the equation. What do they get from referring you?"

"They get to help me out and feel good about it."

"Jen, your clients may feel good about helping you, but that's not the main reason most people will refer you. Besides that, if you have the mindset that asking someone for a referral is asking them to do you a favor or help you out, you may come off as needy. And once someone gives you a referral, you may wind up feeling you owe them. This is one of the main reasons a lot of people don't ask."

Jennifer responded, "I guess you're right. I've always felt that asking for a referral is like asking for a favor. What else could it be?"

"Think about Joe, the contractor who remodeled your kitchen. Last time we met, you said you would refer him in a heartbeat. Why would you refer him?"

"Actually, since we talked, I did refer him to my neighbor." Jennifer smiled and her eyes widened. "I think I'm beginning to connect the dots. I'll tell you why I referred Joe—it was so my neighbor could benefit from my experience and get the same kind of great work he did for me. Guess what? She hired him. And incidentally, I'm glad to see Joe get the business."

Sam exclaimed, "That's it! The main reason most people will refer you is to pay it forward. They want to pass on the positive experience they've had working with you to others they care about. And of course, they'll also be glad to see you get the business."

"Now I get it, Sam."

"Most people are only too willing to let someone else know about a good thing—they just don't always remember to bring it up. That's why you have to ask." Sam paused and took a sip of his margarita. "So how did you feel referring Joe the contractor to your neighbor?"

"I felt really good inside. As you say, it felt like I was paying it forward."

The Love Factor

"It's a win-win-win," said Sam. "Your neighbor wins by getting a great contractor. Joe wins by getting additional work. And you win because you feel good for paying it forward, not to mention the appreciation you get from Joe and your neighbor. You get to be the hero. It's all part of the love factor."

"The love factor? What's that?" asked Jennifer.

"The love factor is the crux of the Referral Code. It's all about the love. I have this saying: There are people who love you

The main reason most people will refer you is to pay it forward. They want to pass on the positive experience they've had working with you to others they care about.

➡

There are people who love you and love the work you do, that have people they love that love them too, who need to love you!

➡

53

and love the work you do, that have people they love that love them too, who need to love you!"

Jennifer started laughing. "No offense, Sam, but all this talk about love sounds a bit 'airy-fairy' for the business world."

Sam responded, "So what do you think relationships are about? They're all about feeling the love. If the love is too gushy for you, call it respect, care, admiration, or appreciation. Like I said, most people are only too willing to let someone else know about a good thing, especially those they respect or care about. Love, goodwill, or whatever you choose to call it, is the emotional currency of business relationships and referrals."

> *Love, goodwill, or whatever you choose to call it, is the emotional currency of business relationships and referrals.*
> ➡

"Now I see what you're saying, Sam. Would you please repeat what you said about the love factor so I can write it down."

Sam repeated, "There are people who love you and love the work you do, that have people they love that love them too, who need to love you!"

When Jennifer was finished writing, Sam continued, "Let's go back to Joe, the contractor. What did you like about working with him, and how did you feel as a result?"

Jennifer didn't have to think about it. "He was an absolute pleasure to work with. I didn't have to worry about a thing. He did a great job and took great care of us. I felt I could leave the whole thing in his hands. I guess you could say I felt well taken care of."

"Great," said Sam. "Now, think about it for a minute—who do you love that loves you, that needs to love Joe too?"

Jennifer thought for a moment, then responded, "Well, there's my coworker who is getting ready for a remodel. I told you about him before. Come to think of it, my Uncle Dave wants to convert his garage into an office. Oh…our friends

Jeannie and Nick just bought a house, and they were talking about knocking down a couple walls to create more space between the living room and the den. I can't believe I didn't think of them before."

Sam replied, "Did you notice that when I asked you who loves you that needs to love Joe too, you came up with two additional people in about twenty seconds? That's the love factor. Don't forget about it. It's an essential aspect of the Referral Code."

Jennifer said, "I'm going to call them all to tell them about Joe."

"Good. Jen, I want you to get this in your bones: People refer based on feelings—the feelings they have for you and the work you do, the feelings they have for those they refer you to, and the feelings they have or as a result of having referred you. People refer based on feelings."

"Sounds like *Sell the Feeling,* Sam."

"It is. As long as we're talking about the love factor, I have some homework for you. Go through your client database and come up with the top five clients who love you and your work the most. Pick clients that you can project have relationships that match your referral type."

People refer based on feelings.

"Will do. Should I go ahead and call them to ask for referrals?"

"Not yet. I've got to teach you when and how to ask."

"Okay, Sam. While we're on the subject of why people would refer me, I've got a concern. Some people may expect that I'll give them a referral fee or some kind of spiff. And some people may want a referral in return. I may be able to do a referral fee sometimes or give some of my clients a referral, but I'm afraid I can't do this for everyone."

"You bring up an important point. If paying a referral fee is legal or acceptable in your business, then you can do it if you choose. But keep in mind that if you give someone a referral fee, it will always be about the fee for that person. The loyalty will last only as long as the money keeps coming.

the referral code

"As far as reciprocating by giving your client a referral, you can do that if you like, but take it from me, it's not necessary. Remember: most people refer you to pay it forward to those they care about. I suggest you put the whole idea of reciprocation out of your mind. If you worry about paying someone back, you may hesitate or even avoid asking for referrals.

"In the rare case that someone comes straight out and asks you for a fee or a reciprocal referral, deal with it on a case-by-case basis. If you are willing to pay a fee, go ahead. If you don't think you can refer the person, be upfront."

"Thanks, Sam. I don't anticipate this kind of thing will happen too often."

"Now we have another key aspect to the nature of the game: why people refer you—how they benefit. This is key, so I want to summarize what we just talked about. By and large, people refer to pay it forward. And once you take care of the people they care about, they get to be the hero. If you get hung up thinking that you are somehow imposing by asking for referrals—that you're asking for a big favor—you may hesitate or come off as needy. When you ask for referrals, you're not asking for help, you are offering to help the people your client cares about."

"It's sinking in, Sam."

"Good. Now, as long as we're here, I'd like to check out the game for a few minutes. Do you mind?"

"No problem, Sam." Jennifer tried to relax and go with Sam's flow.

Sam turned up the volume in their booth. It was the top of the sixth inning and the score was tied one to one. Nothing spectacular happened during the sixth, and Jennifer was getting bored. Beneath the table, she was twiddling her thumbs. Sam noticed her annoyance and waited for her to say something.

After about 10 minutes, Jennifer could no longer restrain herself. "Sam, no offense, but this is just so boring."

"You think so? Let's watch just a little longer. Humor me, okay?"

Jennifer saw that Sam was enjoying himself, so she gave in. Another 15 minutes passed. Not much happened. One runner made it to second and tried to steal third on a fly ball, but the left fielder caught the ball, ending the inning. Jennifer felt herself becoming more restless with each passing minute.

"Sam, why don't you go ahead and finish watching the game. I'll take a cab home and we can take up where we left off next time we meet."

"Just another few minutes, Jen. Just watch with me, okay?"

By now it was the eighth inning. Jennifer ordered another margarita to help pass the time. As she sipped her drink, she stared off into space and wondered why people get so excited about such a tedious sport.

Suddenly, she was startled out of her trance by the sounds of the crowd shouting. A fly ball headed toward the bleachers. In hot pursuit, the right fielder sprinted into action, leapt into the air, and snagged the ball a split second before it could clear the fence.

Then things got quiet again. With the score still tied at the end of the ninth inning, the game went into an extra inning.

Just what I needed, Jennifer thought.

At the bottom of the 10th inning, Jennifer was about to order another drink when a rally started: one man on base, then another, and another. With the bases loaded and the score still tied, the next two batters struck out. The next batter swung twice and let one pass. On the fourth pitch, he connected and knocked the ball out of the park. The crowd in park and the spectators in the bar went wild. Jennifer felt the building shake from the excitement in the main bar downstairs. The game was over.

With a huge grin on his face, Stan exclaimed, "Great game 'eh? This is what it's all about!"

Jennifer glanced across the table at Sam. He was looking at her with a gleam in his eye. After a moment he quipped, "I wonder if this has anything to do with your getting referrals."

the referral code

By now, Jennifer knew that everything with Sam was some kind of lesson. "I think I understand why you made me sit though this, Sam. Are you trying to tell me that if I keep asking people for referrals, I'll eventually score some business?"

"Obviously, persistence is important, but the game represents more than that. To non-fans, the game of baseball often seems slow and uneventful, even boring. The outfielder that caught that fly ball that was headed over the fence saved the game for his team. Though he appeared to be doing very little for nine innings, he was totally alert, focused, and doing the work. He was, what I call, 'patient in the space.'"

Sam continued, "Like the game of baseball, the game of getting referrals requires patience, vigilance, steady work, and pacing. You need to have confidence, maturity, and a sense of mission. Once you ask for referrals, you may experience delays and ambiguous responses. There may be times when it seems as if nothing is happening. There may be times when you ask your clients for referrals and no one comes to mind. You may get bored and be tempted to give up. But if you stay with it, keep the faith, pace yourself, and continue to do the work, you will get a hit—then another, and another. And sooner or later, you will hit a grand slam. I'm certain of it!"

Jennifer took it all in. After a moment, she let out a sigh. "I know I can be impatient, Sam. I always want things to happen right now. In the past, I have missed out on certain opportunities because I wanted the outcome now and wasn't willing pace it out. I just discarded those opportunities and moved on to the next. This is an important lesson for me, Sam. I never thought I would say this, but thanks for making me sit through this baseball game."

"My pleasure. And thanks for your openness. Oh, I almost forgot—I have something for you."

Sam reached in his coat pocket and pulled out a bobble-headed Philadelphia Phillies baseball doll sporting a red hat emblazoned with the letter P.

"This is a reminder, Jen. For you, P stands for patience, pacing, and persistence. Put it on your desk. Anytime you find yourself restless, unfocused, or procrastinating, just tap Phillie's head and remember what we talked about today."

Jennifer tapped the doll's head and burst out laughing. "Thanks for Phillie. He's actually kind of cute." She tapped Phillie's head a couple of more times, each time repeating, "Patience, pacing, persistence."

Leverage

Jennifer asked, "Is there anything else I need to know about the nature of the game?"

"Yes. It's a high-leverage game. Think about cold calling. In most businesses, you have to make a huge number of calls to find anyone interested in your offer. Cold calling is a low-leverage game—lots of outreach and activity to get a single sale. In most businesses, only one to two percent of your calls may produce qualified leads.

"Now think about the Referral Code. The people you approach already know and respect you and your work. They will take your call. Each person you talk to may know several people or organizations that meet your referral type. Suppose you ask 10 people for referrals. Conservatively, each of them knows two people that match your referral type. By having conversations with 10 people, you have potential access to 20. There's a multiplier effect. That's what I call leverage! Compare that with a two-percent hit rate in cold calling. You would have to make a thousand calls to get 20 qualified leads.

"I'm with you, Sam."

"By the way, I know how you feel about cold calling. Personally, I have nothing against cold calling. It is appropriate in certain businesses and in certain circumstances. Some people like to do it and find it very effective. My point is that it's almost always a lower-leverage activity than what you can get through the Referral Code. In most cases, you're better off exhausting your warm referral sources before making cold calls. I have a saying: Warm beats cold every time."

"I like that one, Sam." Jennifer wrote it down.

Sam continued, "Now that you understand more about the nature of the game, let's get back to the scores. Remember that it is never about

Warm beats cold

every time.

the scores until you understand the nature of the game. Then, it's always about the scores. And remember what I said about the love factor and paying it forward.

"Now, how many of your clients do you want to ask for referrals over the next 12 months?" Sam asked again.

This time Jennifer didn't hesitate, "All of them!"

"And what percentage of them do you want to refer you business over the next year?"

Jennifer paused and considered the question. "I'd say 75 percent."

"That's the spirit. You might want to keep score on other things, such as how many referrals you get and how many you convert to sales.

"We've covered a lot of ground today," Sam said. "Next time, we're going to talk about how to have a referral conversation with your clients. Can you meet me at Patty's Diner this Friday at noon?"

"Sounds good to me."

"I'm curious, Jen. What do you take away from this meeting—what stands out for you about the nature of the referral game?"

Jennifer paused for a moment, then gave Sam a big smile. "It's all about the love and paying it forward."

first attempts

When Jennifer got to work the next day, there was an email from Needleman to the sales department:

```
Thanks for the great effort you've contributed to our calling
outreach initiative. Because of the difficult market and
our competitors' aggressive marketing programs, we need
to strengthen our efforts in order to reclaim our industry
leadership position. Effective next week, I am raising the
minimum number of calls from 75 to 90 calls per week. It
represents an average of only 4 extra calls a day. I'm
counting on you to make contact with 20% of the people
you're targeting. Through your efforts, we will get this
ship back on course and sail it into a brighter future.

Best,
Roger
```

Jennifer closed her eyes and bit her tongue to stop from yelling out the expletive that came to mind. As far as she was concerned, Needleman's cold-calling program was useless. It was just busywork. Obviously it wasn't working. Why else would he increase the number of calls? She decided to check in with a coworker to see if his results were any different than hers. She wandered down the hall to Patrick's office.

"How's the cold calling going, Pat?"

"It's a royal pain," replied Patrick. "I've made so many calls that I've got calluses on the ends of my fingers. This is so inefficient. The only meeting I landed was with a company that was price-shopping against their current vendor's renewal contract, which was all but signed. I'm fed up with the whole thing. It may work for some people, but not me.

"Between you and me, Jennifer, I got an offer from another company and I'm giving notice this Friday," Patrick confided. "It's too bad, because I like this place and most of the people.

"If you want my opinion," continued Patrick, "the big brass sees that Needleman's plan is failing, and Needleman is doing the only thing his one-track mind can come up with—if at first you don't succeed, do even more of the same."

Jennifer left Patrick's office dispirited, thinking that she ought to leave too. But the timing wasn't at all right. First, she was still getting paid for renewal business at a time when she and Neil needed the money. And second, she was determined to give the Referral Code system a chance. Once she had proof that it worked, she would approach Needleman and convince him to drop the cold-calling requirements, at least for her.

And there was the matter of the four-thousand-dollar check she wrote to Corky Starr's campaign as a withdrawal penalty. She **had** to see this through.

Jennifer went back to her office and started dialing for dollars. An hour and a half later, she emerged from her office, exasperated. Though she had quit smoking five years earlier, she went outside to the smoking area and bummed a cigarette from a coworker.

After one puff, she stubbed it out. *What the heck am I doing? Why am I letting this get the best of me?*

She walked back to her office to do some more dialing—this time, for referrals, even though Sam had asked her to wait.

She geared up to call one of her best clients. She was a little anxious about asking her client for something. It felt a bit like a role reversal. After all, she was the one there to help meet her clients' needs, not the other way around.

"Hi Gloria, it's Jennifer Stewart from Pacific IT Solutions. How are you?"

Gloria told Jennifer she was glad she called. Gloria's company was having a service issue: one of their servers was down and they had sent in a request for a service call. Six hours later, they were still waiting for a return call. Jennifer put Gloria on-hold and made a call. When she came back to Gloria, she told her that someone would be out within the hour.

"Thanks for taking care of this," said Gloria. "I was beginning to get worried. When we signed on with you guys, you guaranteed immediate response time to our support issues."

"Gloria, I am so sorry you had to wait. Our help desk said that your request was somehow misrouted. This is a rare occurrence, a complete fluke. I assure you it will not happen again. You can always call me directly if there's ever an issue."

"Thanks, Jennifer. I really appreciate your stepping in. By the way, what was the reason you called?"

Jennifer launched her first referral request, "I wanted to ask you—uh, for a favor. If you know of anyone that could use our services, I would really appreciate an introduction."

Gloria responded, "No one comes to mind at the moment, but let me think about it and ask around. I'll get back to you as soon as I hear anything."

"Thanks, Gloria. That would be great."

Jennifer felt somewhat relieved that she had asked and that Gloria had given her positive indications. She realized that she had accidentally framed her request as a favor, but it didn't matter. After all, Gloria said she would ask around. She imagined that Gloria knew a lot of people. It sounded promising.

Jennifer picked up the phone and called another client, Max. She and Max chatted for a couple of minutes, all the while Jennifer working up the nerve to ask. Finally, she found an opening.

"Max, you know the changes in the market have caused some of our clients to put their plans for expansion on hold. I'm looking to find some new companies we can help. Do you know of anyone I should be talking to?"

the referral code

"Let me think about it." A few seconds went by. "I need to think about it some more. I'll look through my database and call you back if I get any ideas."

"Thanks Max."

Jennifer felt pretty good. This was so much better than cold calling. After all, these were her clients. They knew her company, liked her, and could recommend her to the people they knew.

They seemed like they genuinely want to help me. That's a good start.

Then she remembered what Sam said: The Referral Code isn't about your clients helping **you**—it's about them helping others they care about that need what you do or have. It's about paying it forward.

So let them pay it forward. Let's see what happens.

the referral conversation

Jennifer was excited to tell Sam the good news: she asked two of her clients for referrals and both said they would be happy to refer her if they thought of anyone who might be suitable. She had 'jumped ahead of the class,' but she doubted Sam would mind since she had taken the initiative and her results were promising.

When Jennifer arrived at Patty's Diner, Sam already had a table. He asked her how Neil was doing.

"He's improving and walking much better. I just can't wait until he gets that wire contraption off his jaw. I want to hear his voice again."

"Give him my best. Tell him I'll stop by and see him later this week."

After they placed their orders, Jennifer said, "I've been looking forward to today, Sam. You promised to show me how to ask for referrals."

Sam began, "Yes, we'll get to that. But before we do, I have a question for you. Why haven't you asked your clients for referrals up until now?"

"Actually, I just did," Jennifer answered with a self-satisfied grin.

"Oh really? I want to hear what happened, but not just yet. Why haven't you asked in the past?"

"I'm not entirely sure. It just never occurred to me to ask."

"Never? An ambitious go-getter like you? How come?"

Jennifer thought about the question before answering, "I have to admit, it was uncomfortable for me to ask because it seemed awkward—like a role-reversal. I'm here to service my clients' needs, not the other way around. But now I see that it's not about asking them for help—I'm looking for the opportunity to help the people they know and care about. And in the process, they get to be the hero for referring me. It's a win-win-win, right?"

"You got it!"

"To be entirely honest with you, Sam, I think there's another reason I've been uncomfortable. I don't want to come off as desperate for business."

"You've got a lot of company, Jen. A lot of people would love to get referrals, but they don't ask because they're afraid of being seen as needy."

Sam went on, "I've found that people don't ask for referrals for a number of reasons. First, most people don't know **how to ask**. There are several ways to ask. Some work better than others, and some rarely work at all.

"Second, is not knowing **when to ask**. Timing is important—it can make the difference between someone actually referring you or shuffling your request to the 'to-do-later' pile. Once it's in that pile, good luck—that pile is a direct detour to the 'land of lost intentions.'"

Fear is the ultimate wet blanket—it can kill initiative, if you let it.

Jennifer chuckled. "Where do you come up with this stuff, Sam?"

"Observation and experience," Sam said with a twinkle in his eye. "Third—and this is the big one—like you, many people are **afraid to ask**. Fear is the ultimate wet blanket—it can kill initiative, if you let it."

The Three Ugly Sisters: Pushy, Needy, and Rejected

Sam added, "In my experience, three fears stop people from asking for referrals. I call them the 'Three Ugly Sisters.'"

Jennifer burst out laughing, "Please tell me more."

"People have three fears about asking for referrals. They're afraid they will come off as pushy. Second, like you, they're afraid of being seen as needy. Third, they're afraid that if they ask for referrals and don't get them, they will feel rejected. So meet the three ugly sisters: Pushy, Needy, and Rejected."

Jennifer replied, "Unfortunately, I already know them well. I've got to admit that I've had every one of those fears."

"So have a lot of people. Some people over-dramatize this whole business of asking, like an awkward teenager getting ready to ask a girl for a date." Sam put on a goofy grin and did his best imitation of a sixteen-year-old boy whose voice was starting to change, "How do I ask Mary Jane to the prom? Is now a good time, or is it too early? I don't want to seem too eager. Oh my God, what if she says no? What if she doesn't like me?"

Jennifer laughed and Sam continued in his normal voice, "Many people make the idea of asking for referrals too much about **themselves**. Remember: you're not asking for a handout. You are offering your clients a chance to **pay it forward**, so you can help people they know and care about. Asking for referrals is not a sign of neediness or weakness—it is a sign of **strength**. Now why don't you go ahead and tell me about the referral conversations you had with your clients."

Jennifer told Sam about the two clients she called. When she was done, she said. "I feel pretty good about how it went. They both seemed very agreeable about referring me, and said they would think about it and get back to me. One of them even said she would ask around. Good start, don't you think?"

Sam sat back, paused for a moment, then replied, "Hats off to you for asking. It's good that you broke through your resistance. With all due respect, though, I will be surprised if they get back to you."

"What do you mean?" Jennifer was visibly rattled. "I have good relationships with both of these clients. They said they would get back to me."

"When?"

"I don't know. They didn't say."

"Did you ask?"

"No. I didn't want to put them on the spot or pressure them."

"Jen, it's not about pressure. Remember, these people love you and the work you do. They may be perfectly willing to refer you. They may even intend to do so, but like a lot of people, they may be busy with the clutter of their own lives and they need your follow-up to remind them. Think about it: how often have you intended to do something, but you let the circumstances drive your intentions into oblivion? My guess is that your clients will get busy and forget about your request.

"By the time we're done today, you will understand what was missing from your conversation. Once you grasp the fundamentals of the referral conversation, you can go back ask them again.

"So are you ready, Jen?"

"I guess I am."

Just then the waitress arrived with their food and said, "You two look so engrossed in your conversation. I was going to wait for an opening, but I didn't want your lunch to get cold."

Sam turned to Jennifer. "Food is so much better **warm**, just like business leads, wouldn't you agree?"

Jennifer laughed, "You're relentless, Sam."

The Passive Approach

When the waitress left, Sam continued, "There are two basic approaches to the referral conversation. I call them the **active approach** and the **passive approach**. Most people take the passive approach. That's what you did."

Jennifer cringed and shot back defensively, "Passive? What are you talking about? I came right out and asked them!"

"I didn't say **you** were passive," Sam replied. "However, your approach didn't call for any direct action on their part or yours. You basically left the ball in their court to scout referrals with no plan as to what happens next. I have a question for you: at this point, who is in charge of the game? You or the people you asked? Who has the ball?"

"I guess they do."

"That's what I mean by passive. Many people use the passive approach to soften their request because they're afraid of being seen as pushy."

"Well you've got that right—I **was** concerned about being pushy."

Sam continued, "Let's talk about the passive approach. There are few varieties. The most passive of all is what I call the **organic approach**: you hope or expect referrals to come to you naturally just because you provide great products or services. In other words, the organic approach assumes that you shouldn't have to ask.

"The problem with the organic approach is that it is an illusion. It simply does not reflect the way the world works.

"With the organic approach, the referrals, if they come, will be few and far between. Remember: only about five percent of people are natural promoters who will refer you without being asked. I have a buddy who believed in the organic approach. His clientele nearly dropped to zero. I got him to start asking, and his business turned around. Like I said before, **you have to ask**."

Jennifer said, "Ask and you shall receive."

"That's right. Another variety of the passive approach is what I call the **if-then request**. Most people who ask for referrals use this approach. The if-then request goes something like this: Jennifer, **if** you think of someone who could use my services, **then** please let me know or have them call me.

"The **when-then request** is similar to if-then. **When** you run across someone who could use my services, **then** please don't hesitate to give them my number."

Jennifer responded, "That sounds like what I did. What's wrong with that?"

the referral code

"Both of these approaches lack specificity; they have no explicit call to action and no plan for follow-up. The if-then request reminds me of the kid asking for a date. It sounds something like this," Sam said, transitioning back to his teenage-boy voice. "Mary Jane, I was wondering, if you don't have anything to do, would you maybe like to go to a movie or something, sometime?"

Sam continued, "When you make an if-then or when-then request, you may feel like you're being proactive, but it probably won't get you what you want, because it relies on the person you ask getting around to it. This iffy approach is just too circumstantial. If you make an iffy request, the results will be iffy."

Jennifer looked down, shook her head in frustration, and let out a sigh.

"Don't get me wrong, Jen. Sometimes the if-then request does work. It's better than nothing. At least you asked. That's a lot better than some people do."

"Thanks, Sam."

Sam went on, "Another variety of the passive approach is asking for referrals on a feedback form. I'm sure you've seen this. A vendor asks you to provide feedback about your experience. They might ask what they can improve or what you didn't like about their service. Then they ask if you'd be willing to refer them in the future. They may even ask you to list names of people that might be interested what they offer. Why on earth would you ask for referrals on the same form where you ask what could be improved or what didn't work? It makes no sense whatsoever! Think about it, Jen: when you give someone feedback about what didn't work for you, you're not going to be in a positive state about them."

Jennifer chimed in, "I see your point."

"And here's my favorite example of the passive approach. I've been saving this for you," said Sam, pulling his cell phone from his pocket to show Jen a text message:

To our valued patients: Our greatest honor is to receive your referrals. Please do not hesitate to refer us to your family and friends.

—Maxwell & Marks Dental Associates

"For crying out loud," said Sam. "Do they really think that sending out a message like this will get them referrals? What on earth are they thinking? People will see that message and instantly delete it from their phone and their mind. It's a nuisance and the ultimate in passivity!"

"I get what you're saying about the passive approach, Sam. What's the active approach?"

When to Ask

"We're about to get to that. Before we do, I have a question for you. When do you think is the best time to ask for referrals?"

"I guess the best time is when the other person is in a good mood, but I know that leaves it up to circumstances. When is the best time to ask?"

"It is about the person being in a positive state, Jen, but you don't have to leave it up to the circumstances."

Sam continued, "Last time we were together I asked you what you liked so much about working with your contractor. You told me a number of things that you liked about him. Then I asked you who else you knew that needed to love him too. Do you remember what happened next?"

"Sure, I do. I realized I could refer Joe to my Uncle Dave and our friends Jeannie and Nick."

"You came up with two new potential referrals, right then and there. I'm curious—how did you do that?"

"You asked me who I knew and I came up with them."

"When did I ask you?"

"Right after I told you what I liked so much about working with Joe."

"So you were in a state of appreciation about Joe and his services, weren't you?"

"Absolutely."

"That, my friend, is the best time to ask: when your client is in a **state of appreciation** about you or your services or products."

The best time to ask:

When your client is in

a state of appreciation

about you or your

services or products.

➡

"That makes total sense, Sam."

"Of course, it does. It's amazing how few people put this to use. Let me tell you a story about my granddaughter. Kate is four and very bright. Last month, I was visiting Kate, my daughter, and my son-in-law. One night, Kate was alone in her room while we were talking in the kitchen. We went in to check on her, and her room was completely clean. All her toys and books were on the shelves. Apparently this was unusual. Her dad asked her who put everything away. She gave him a big grin and said she did it all herself. He said, 'Honey, it's awesome that you cleaned up your room without being asked. Thank you so much!'

"Without missing a beat, Kate said, 'Daddy, can I have **two** cookies?'"

Jennifer chuckled, and Sam continued, "What do you think her dad did? He didn't say, 'I'll think about it and get back to you.' He gave her the two cookies right then and there, enthusiastically. Kids are smart. Kate instinctively recognized that Daddy was in a state of appreciation and knew that the time was right. She asked him for not one, but **two** cookies. What a great way to ask for a referral!"

"Great story, Sam, but how do I put this to use? I know my clients appreciate me, but honestly, if I have to sit around and wait until they are feeling the love, I may have to wait a long time. Most of our conversations are touch-and-go—about day-to-day business and service issues."

Sam replied, "Haven't there have been times when a client tells you what a great job you've done or how much they appreciate your services?"

"Sure."

"That's a **naturally occurring state of appreciation** and a great cue for you to ask for referrals right then and there. Pay attention to these cues when they come up, then ask. I'll show you how in a minute, but before I forget, there's something I want to mention: You took an unnecessary risk when you asked the client with the service problem for referrals. Granted, you did take action to resolve her complaint before you asked her, but I would have waited until the service issue was handled. Then you could have called her to make sure everything was satisfactory. If she expressed appreciation, that would have been the time to ask."

"Oops—my bad. I'll call her tomorrow and make sure she feels taken care of."

"Good, and if she's in a state of appreciation, you can remind her about your request and ask her who comes to mind.

"Back to your question about waiting until someone feels the love—you don't have to wait for a naturally occurring state of appreciation, you can actually evoke it."

"I can? How?"

The Active Approach

Sam leaned forward and put both hands on the table.

"Okay, Jen. Now we're ready to talk about the **active approach** to asking for referrals. Usually, you will want to have the conversation in-person, but you can do it over the phone, if necessary."

Step 1 – Ask the State-Evoker Question

"The first thing is to make sure the other person is in a state of appreciation. You can do this by asking what I call the **state-evoker question**. It's a great way to initiate the referral conversation. Listen carefully—here's the state-evoker question:

Jen, what are some of the things that have worked for you in our working together?

"Go ahead and answer, Jen."

Jennifer thought for a moment and responded, "Well, Sam, I like your whole approach—the way you're coaching me to succeed at getting more qualified referrals. I'm impressed with your knowledge and wisdom. Most of all I like that you care so much, and I'm so grateful." Jennifer started to tear up a bit.

"Good. Are you in a state of appreciation?"

Wiping her eyes, Jennifer said, "Yes, can't you tell?"

"Yes. By the way, thanks—I appreciate your appreciation."

Just then, Patty entered the dining area and spotted Sam and Jennifer. She walked over to their table.

"Sam, it's lovely to see you again. And I see you brought your friend back. Good to see you, Jennifer. Sam, I can't tell you how much I appreciate that you've introduced so many of your friends to us. You're a blessing."

Sam blushed. "My pleasure, Patty. You know me—when I find a good thing, I like to shout it from the rooftops. Patty, as long as you're here, there's something I've been meaning to talk to you about. I'm on the board of directors of our local food bank. We feed homeless and hungry people all over the city. Last year, we distributed over 300,000 meals. We're conducting our annual pledge drive, and I wonder if you would be willing to help us feed some of the unfortunate souls living on the streets."

"I am delighted to help, Sam. Thanks for asking me."

Sam gave Patty the details on how to donate, and she disappeared into the back office.

Jennifer smiled and said, "It's wonderful that you're involved with the food bank. Talk about timing. Patty was in a naturally occurring state of appreciation, right?"

Sam smiled back and nodded, "Like I said, it's the best time to ask."

A few moments later, Patty returned to the table, placed a folded check into Sam's hand, patted it, and said, "You can always count on me to support your causes, Sam. I am honored to help feed people in need—after all, I've dedicated my life to feeding others."

Without looking at the check, Sam put it into his shirt pocket and thanked Patty.

After Patty left, Jennifer said, "Aren't you curious about how much she gave?"

"I'll look later. Let's continue with our discussion."

Jennifer asked, "So what do I do after asking the state-evoker question?"

"Listen carefully. Your client will tell you what he values in your working together—how he perceives the benefits of your working relationship. Make a mental note of what he says—his keywords and phrases. Write them down if that helps.

"And while you listen, use your sensory awareness to detect any signs of a state change. You should notice some kind of shift as he answers your question. It may be a change of tone or pacing in his speech; it may be a color shift in his face or a smile. You are looking for a shift, no matter how subtle, that indicates that your client is going into a state of appreciation.

"If you don't detect a change of state, or if you think the person may have more to say, you may need to 'stack the state.' You can ask, 'What are some **other** things that have worked for you in our working together?' Or, 'What about that worked for you?'"

Step 2 – Ask for the Referral

"Once your client is in a state of appreciation, whether it's naturally occurring or a result of the state-evoker question, it's time to ask for referrals. This is where most people use the passive approach, like you did—something like, 'If you know of anyone who could use our services, then please don't hesitate to give them my name.'

"With the active approach, you ask them **who** they know that meets your referral type, right then and there. Instead of asking **if** they know someone or **when** they run across someone, you want to ask **who** they know. The question is:

Who do you know [then give your referral type] **that can benefit from the same kind of service (or product) you experienced, like what you said** [then give the benefits they just told you]**?**

Sam continued, "Remember when you told me why you appreciate me and my services? One of the things you mentioned was my coaching you to succeed in your business by getting more referrals. Here's how I'd frame the referral question: Jennifer, who do you know that's a high-level producer like you that can benefit from the same kind of service you experienced, like coaching you to succeed at getting more qualified referrals?

"Alternatively, you can put your referral type at the end of the question, like this: Jennifer, who do you know that can benefit from the same kind of service you experienced, like coaching you to succeed at getting more qualified referrals—someone that's a high-level producer?

When Jennifer finished taking notes, she said, "This is really different. I would have never thought of doing it this way."

Sam quipped, "You've got to do something different if you want different results. If you keep doing more of the same, you'll get what you've always gotten.

"I want to point out something about the referral question," said Sam. "The question, 'Who do you know?' is an open-ended question and calls for a response—specifically, a name or names. Notice how that differs from, 'If you know someone, please don't hesitate to refer me.' That's not even a question, and it doesn't call for an immediate response. Instead, you will likely get a response like, 'Sure, I'll be glad to refer you if I ever run into someone who needs your services.'

"Some people ask, 'Do you know anyone who could use my services?' This is called a closed-ended question. It calls for an answer like, yes, no, or not at the moment. Always use the open-ended question, 'Who do you know...,' when asking for referrals."

Jennifer replied, "Point taken. Sam, I'm curious, did you come up with all this? Where did it come from?"

"That's a whole other story, Jen. I'll tell it to you someday. We've got more to cover now."

Sam continued, "Let's pretend that you're meeting with a client. How do you think one of your clients might respond to the state-evoker question, 'What are some of the things that have worked for you in our working together?'"

Always use the open-ended question, 'Who do you know...,' when asking for referrals.

"I think they would say that our team is very responsive, we keep their entire operation running smoothly with minimal down-time, we provide them with cost-effective solutions about hardware and software, and they know they can depend on us 24/7."

"Great," said Sam. "Keeping that in mind, how would you ask the referral question?"

Jennifer looked at her notes as she framed the question. "Sam, who do you know in a company with at least two hundred people that can benefit from the same kind of service you've experienced, like the responsiveness, cost-effectiveness, and 24/7 dependability?"

"Perfect, Jen—you've got it!"

"That wasn't so hard."

"Of course is wasn't. It's just a question. By the way, some people are a little uncomfortable asking the referral question because they feel it's a bit too direct. If you want, you can soften it by saying, 'Jack, I was wondering, who do you know...?'

"I like that."

"One more thing. Once you ask the referral question, **don't** say anything until your client answers. Some people get anxious and keep talking. It's similar to asking a closing question in selling—once you ask the question, shut up and wait for a response."

"Thanks, Sam. I'll remember that."

Step 3 – Handle the Response

Sam continued, "Next comes handling the response. Once you ask the referral question, you will get one of two responses. Hopefully, the client will tell you they know someone. Sometimes, they will say that they can't think of anyone in that moment."

"That's what happened with my clients last week," said Jennifer. "What do I do if someone says they'll think about it?"

"Just say, 'No problem. Why don't I check in with you in a week or so and see who has come to mind?' Then call the person back in about a week, and say, 'Remember our conversation last week? I wanted to check in with you and see who has come to mind.' If they tell you that they haven't had a chance to think about it, you can say, 'No problem, why don't I check in with you again in a week or so.' Then try again. Alternatively, you can mention some industries you work with and ask them right then and there who comes mind."

"Sounds pretty straightforward."

"It is, but remember this: When you say you are going to follow up with someone in a week or so, put it in your calendar and be sure to keep your word. For most people, 'a week or so' means seven to 10 days. Don't wait any longer than that. If you do, your request may be forgotten or the other person may take it that you don't keep your word.

"One more thing: You may have to keep at it—some people who are perfectly willing to refer you, need to be reminded, sometimes two or three times."

Jennifer asked, "Suppose someone has a referral for me—do I get the person's info or should I have my client contact them first?"

"Both. Let's say Jack wants to refer you to Jill. I suggest you say, 'Why don't I go ahead and take down Jill's number.' If Jack hasn't told you anything about Jill, ask some questions so you can qualify the lead. That way, you'll have a context when you call her. But don't call her yet."

"Why not?"

"This is a **warm lead-generating system**. The lead will be much stronger if your client qualifies the lead and warms it up for you. That's one of the key things that makes this system so effective."

"How do I get my client to qualify the lead and warm it up?"

"Say, 'Thanks, Jack. I'm wondering if you can go ahead and give Jill a call to introduce me and let her know what's worked for you in our working together.' It's usually best if Jack calls Jill, but some people may prefer to introduce you by email. If so, ask them to copy you.

"Once Jack agrees to call Jill, you want to make sure that he follows through and that she is expecting your call. Just ask Jack, 'When do you think you'll have a chance to contact Jill?' Suppose Jack says, 'I'll call her sometime next week.' You would respond, 'Great. I'll follow up with you then to make sure it's okay to call her.'"

"I'm catching on, Sam. I'll put it in my calendar and be sure to follow up with Jack.

"I have a question," Jennifer added. "What if someone says they don't know anyone?"

You may have to keep at it—some people who are perfectly willing to refer you, need to be reminded, sometimes two or three times.

"They might know someone who knows others who meet your referral type. This is called a **referral source referral**. If they do not know anyone directly, you could ask, 'Who do you know that trusts you and is connected to companies that I can help?'"

"I didn't realize my relationships can refer me to other referral sources. That's intriguing."

Sam smiled and said, "The richness of our relationships can lead us to more riches."

The richness of our relationships can lead us to more riches.

Jennifer said, "I like that, Sam. Once I follow up with Jack to make sure he has connected with Jill, I'm done with the referral conversation, right?"

Step 4 – Ask for More Cookies

"Not so fast. If you were to stop there, you run the real risk of leaving referrals on the table. I strongly suggest you ask for two cookies, or even more."

"What do you mean?"

"If my granddaughter did it, I see no reason you can't. As long as Jack is in a state of appreciation, he may have more people that he loves that love him that need to love you! Once again, you need to ask."

"I'm game. How do I ask him?"

"Once you've established that you're going to follow up with Jill, just ask, 'Who else comes to mind?' Remember what Wayne Gretzky said: 'You miss 100 percent of the shots you don't take.' If you don't ask, you may leave referrals on the table. If you leave referrals on the table, you may be leaving business on the table. If you leave business on the table, you may be leaving money on the table."

"Alright already, I get it, Sam. So once I ask for another cookie, then what?"

"Keep asking for cookies until Jack runs out. You'll know when it's time to stop."

Step 5 (Optional) – Acknowledge Your Referral Partner

"Once Jack has given you a referral, you may want to acknowledge him. Of course you'll thank him, but I'm talking about something more."

"Do you mean I should give him a gift or something like that?"

"You could do that later, especially if the referral turns into business. It's up to you. But I'm talking about something that is in the moment. Once your client gives you the name of someone to talk to, you say, 'Thanks, Jack. You know one of the things I appreciate in our working together is...' Then you tell Jack what you appreciate about working with **him**. This acknowledgement is a nice touch, kind of like the cherry on the top of an ice cream sundae. You don't have to do it, but it can be helpful because it keeps the feeling of appreciation circulating."

Sam continued, "If you are going to acknowledge Jack, don't make it up on the fly. Before you have the referral conversation with Jack, make sure you think about what you appreciate about working with him so you'll know what to say."

Just then, a waitress arrived at their table carrying a pie. "Would y'all like a slice of homemade banana cream pie, on the house?"

"We sure would," Sam answered.

After her first bite, Jennifer said, "You know Sam, one of the things I appreciate about our working together is that good food is always involved."

Step 6 – Contact the Referral

After they finished their pie, Sam continued, "Once you've made sure that Jack has contacted Jill and that she is expecting your call, it's time to contact her. The timing here is essential. Once Jack gives you the go-ahead to call Jill, do it as soon as possible. Do not wait any longer than two or three days. Any longer and you run the risk of breeching trust with Jack, and Jill may wonder what is taking you so long. Plus if you delay, it may reflect poorly on Jack in Jill's eyes."

the referral code

"Do I do anything special when I call Jill?"

"Just introduce yourself, tell her that Jack referred you, then ask questions to establish the need for your services, and arrange a meeting once you've qualified the need. In other words, sell the feeling. Once you talk to Jill, you have one thing left to do."

"What's that?"

"Contact Jack and tell him you talked with Jill. You can tell him a bit about the result. No matter what happened, tell Jack it was a great referral and how much you appreciate it. You can do this by phone, letter, or email—use your judgment as to what's best for Jack. That's it. Any questions?"

"I'm sure I'll come up with some, once I digest this lesson…and the pie. I am so full—my stomach and my brain."

Sam said, "We've come to a good stopping point. I've got some homework for you. Have the referral conversation with at least three of the people on your top-five list. I also suggest that once another week has elapsed you follow up with the two people you already talked with see if they have come up with anyone. If not, ask the state-evoker question and start the whole process over with them."

"Okay, Sam. Thanks so much. I don't mean to pry, but I'm curious about the check Patty gave you."

Sam took the check out of his shirt pocket, unfolded it, and placed it on the table.

Jennifer exclaimed, "$2,500 dollars! Congratulations, Sam! I'm sure that will feed a lot of people."

"This is great! Yes, it will feed a lot of people. You can reach a lot of people, if you know when and how to ask."

"I want to give you a donation, too," said Jennifer.

She brought out her checkbook and wrote a $500 check to the food bank.

"Thank you so much for your generosity, Jen. I'm touched."

"You're welcome. You know, Sam, one of the things I appreciate about our working together is the way you see opportunities to pay it forward."

"Thanks, Jen. In my experience, that's what a good life is all about: **paying it forward.**"[1]

shut up, focus up, and do the work!

➜

hat night, Jennifer told Neil about Sam's lesson on the referral conversation. Neil smiled and wrote on his chalkboard, *Love it!*

She also told him about the Three Ugly Sisters: Pushy, Needy, and Rejected. When he heard the name, Three Ugly Sisters, Neil broke out laughing. Because his jaw was wired shut, Neil's laugh sounded nasal and muffled, which caused Jennifer to melt into a fit of laughter. Of course, this caused Neil to laugh even more.

When their laughter died down, Neil wrote, *What's your fear?* He looked Jennifer in the eye, earnestly awaiting her answer.

Jennifer was not one to admit weakness of any kind. But something about Neil's sincere expression, combined with his injury, led her to open up.

"To tell you the truth, I have all three fears to some degree," she told him. "I know some people think I have a strong personality. I'm concerned that by being so direct in asking for referrals, some folks will see me as a 'pushy bitch.' You know how much I hate that image. At the same time, I'm afraid they'll see me as needy. And quite frankly, with this slowdown in business and Needleman breathing down my neck about cold calling, I **do** feel needy. And what if I go to all the trouble to have the referral conversation with my clients and I get rejected? I hate that feeling more than anything!"

Neil listened carefully, then gave Jennifer a knowing nod. He picked up his chalkboard and wrote, *Talk 2 Sam re: rejection!*

the referral code

Later that evening, Jennifer and Neil got into bed, turned on the TV, and Neil began his nightly ritual: flipping through the cable news channels. Reports about the faltering economy dominated the news. Pundit after pundit lamented the current state of affairs and predicted worse things to come. Jennifer felt herself sinking into a morass of doom-and-gloom. To make things worse, Neil landed on a channel that was airing a campaign ad for her former schoolmate, Corky Starr.

"Oh my God—not Corky! Give me that thing!" Jennifer wrested the remote control from Neil's grasp and found a nice Tracy and Hepburn movie to soothe her anxiety.

The next morning, Jennifer skimmed through several online news sites and blogs and encountered more dire predictions about business and the economy. The more she read, the more distressed she became. She developed a queasy sensation in the pit of her stomach and tension in her neck.

Holy crap! This is scary stuff, she thought, imagining a number of doomsday scenarios, each of which had a devastating effect on her future.

Over breakfast, she opened up her bag of fears to Neil, "Business is drying up everywhere. How am I supposed to get referrals, not to mention business, in this environment? Everyone is scared. People are not going to put their attention on referring me. And even if I do get a referral, nobody is buying! What a crap storm!"

Neil grabbed his chalkboard and wrote, *Honey, becuz I love u...*

Jennifer braced herself. "Honey, because I love you" was a code phrase she and Neil used before delivering an important message the other might not want to hear.

Neil erased his board and wrote, *Shut up, focus up, and do the work!*

Jennifer shot Neil a dirty look. After a moment of consideration, she softened. "Thanks, honey. That's good advice, and I needed to hear it."

But soon after she said it, her inner demons countered, *Fat chance anything I do will make a difference in **this** market!*

three strikes

Jennifer's gyrations over the 'economic crap storm' persisted for the next three days. She consumed the media coverage and put herself into a state of anxiety, uncertainty, and doubt. She fed herself antacids for her nervous stomach and aspirin for her stiff neck. On the job, she consumed herself with busywork and cold calling (with disappointing results). She procrastinated for two days before starting her homework for Sam: three referral conversations.

On Day Three, she arrived at work determined to dig in. She received an email with a link to a video clip of an economist whose forecast sent a shiver down her spine. She felt 'the funk'—a nagging state of negativity, anxiety, and doubt—creep in. Then she reminded herself of Neil's advice: *Shut up, focus up, and do the work*!

Jennifer looked at the list of her top five clients and decided to start with Rita Rauche, vice president of technical operations for a local chain of banks. She considered Rita one of her best clients. Jennifer's company had proposed and implemented a sizeable IT infrastructure improvement plan that had saved the bank considerable time and money. She worked closely with Rita on the plan and knew that the results helped Rita look like a hero to the higher-ups.

Jennifer realized that Rita was extremely busy and decided it was best to have the conversation on the phone rather than in-person. Rita was a real get-to-the-point communicator, so Jennifer decided to skip the state-evoker question and go straight to the referral question.

"Rita, who do you know in a company with at least two hundred people that can benefit from our services?"

the referral code

Rita paused for a moment and replied, "I don't really know of anyone right now. Frankly, Jennifer, I'm so busy I can't really give this the attention you deserve. I will call you if I think of anyone."

That was an icy blow-off, Jennifer thought. *And after all I've done for her!*

Because Jennifer was upset about the 'icy blow-off,' she went back to cold calling and made no further referral calls that day.

The next day, Jennifer hunkered down and called another of her top five, Rick Hancock, the COO of a mortgage company. The receptionist told her that Rick was no longer at the company and asked if she wanted to speak to his replacement's assistant. Jennifer declined.

Another casualty of this damn market, she told herself, even though she had no real information on Rick's departure. She had his mobile phone number, but decided not to call. *I'm sure the last thing he needs now is for me to call him and ask for referrals.* She felt the funk creep up on her again.

Shut up, focus up, and do the work! Neil's words came back to her and pulled her out of her doldrums. She decided to call her client Nancy Hellman, the IT director for Newfield Temp, an agency that provided short-term office workers. Newfield's service contract was coming up for renewal in a couple months, and Jennifer thought she could kill two birds with one stone: check with Nancy on her future service needs and ask her for referrals. Jennifer scheduled a meeting the next day at Nancy's office.

The next day, Nancy kept Jennifer waiting for nearly half an hour.

"I'm so sorry," said Nancy when she finally emerged from the conference room. "We just had a budget meeting, and it lasted way longer than expected. As you can imagine, so many issues are related to the cutbacks in business spending. What a headache!"

Nancy spent the next several minutes bemoaning the setbacks her company was facing. Again, Jennifer felt the funk creep in.

When they finally got down to business, Nancy said that she was very pleased with the service Jennifer and her team had provided over the past year. They would definitely renew the contract, but because of mandatory across-the-board budget cuts, they might need to cut back some of the services.

Jennifer responded, "We can certainly analyze this and determine what is best for you."

Nancy continued lamenting the current market. As the conversation progressed, Jennifer looked for an opening to initiate the referral conversation. She remembered that Sam had stressed the importance of the client's state. Nancy had just come from a depressing meeting and was stressing over the future. Why have the referral conversation with her now? Feeling deflated, Jennifer decided to postpone the conversation to a more opportune time.

Even though she believed it would have been the wrong time to ask, Jennifer launched into a negative head spin: *Did I chicken out? This is a hell of a time for me to ask anyone for referrals. I made the three calls and have nothing to show. That's three strikes—I'm out. This will never work. I wonder what kind of cutbacks Nancy will have to make. What if all my clients cut back? Maybe Neil and I should cut our expenses even more. I better not buy that pair of shoes.*

And on she went, her worried thoughts and speculations sailing off into the void.

get beyond yourself

a fter her 'third strike,' Jennifer spent the rest of the day listlessly dialing for dollars. She was scheduled to meet Sam at his home after work. She decided to reschedule their meeting because she had no positive results to report. The last thing she wanted to do was face Sam while she was feeling so low and out of control. She reached for the phone to call Sam, then noticed Phillie on her desk. She tapped his head, and as it began to bob, she remembered the message: patience, pacing, persistence.

Okay, what the hell—I'll go meet Sam.

On the drive to Sam's house, Jennifer entertained thoughts of quitting her job and ditching the whole Referral Code system. Then she saw a newly posted billboard a few blocks from Sam's house: *Corky Starr for State Assembly— When the old ways aren't working, it's time for a change!* She felt her blood begin to boil.

Sam invited her in, and they sat down at his kitchen table.

"How's it going with your top five?" Sam asked.

"I'm afraid my batting average hasn't been good, Sam. You might say I've struck out."

"That's hardly something **I** would say. I'm curious—why would **you** say it?"

Jennifer took a deep breath and let it out, "Sam, I'm not getting anywhere. I don't know how I can build any business in this market. Many of my clients are cutting back and some are facing layoffs. Neil told me I should just shut up, focus up, and do the work, but what good will it do when **no one** is buying?"

the referral code

For the next several minutes, Jennifer dumped her tribulations onto Sam. She wailed over the 'economic crap storm' and the distressing news on TV and the Internet.

Sam took it all in, and when Jennifer was finished, he responded, "Jen, how come you've chosen to buy into this massive societal trance?"

"What do you mean by societal trance? Haven't you seen the news lately? The economy is crashing!"

"I'm quite aware of the challenges in the current economic environment," said Sam. "However, I refuse to waste my time and energy listening to talking heads and fear mongers. Why would you give even a fraction of your attention to anyone who sells sensationalism, negativity, and fear? Sure, the economy is in trouble. But dwelling on it only takes you down—down to the level of the masses who are wringing their hands in the air, as if the world were coming to an end."

"Well, it **is** bad."

"Yes, business is down, but do you know what's going to turn it around?"

"More government bailouts? I'm not sure what's going to turn it around."

"Regardless of what the government does, I'll tell you what's ultimately going to turn things around: people who have the presence of mind, the guts, and a plan to go out there and build more business. They are the ones with foresight. The naysayers and doom-and-gloomers only make matters worse. Which camp do you want to be in?"

Jennifer forced a smile. "The former, obviously. That's why I'm working with you."

"Then you've got to get out of your own head and stop marinating in the poison juices of your negative thoughts. You've got to get beyond yourself."

Jennifer closed her eyes and nodded.

"Listen, Jen, this market will turn around. They always do. Do you think anyone wins in a down market?

"Sure they do."

"Well then why not **you**?"

"That's a good question—why **not** me?"

"I like what Neil said, 'Shut up, focus up, and do the work!' He's quite a wise man, that husband of yours. I wonder where he learned so much?"

Sam gave Jennifer a playful grin, then added, "Jen, once you really buckle down and consistently do the work, things will start to shift in your world. But you absolutely must take control of your mental game. Remember what I said about patience and persistence. During market slowdowns, many professionals stress out and go off their game. If you intentionally focus your efforts now, you'll be way ahead when the market shifts. While others are tearing their hair out, you'll be building something."

Shut up, focus up,

and do the work!

➤

"How do I get control of my mental game when times seem so rotten, Sam?"

"First, you must realize just how important your mindset is, always, but **especially** at a time when most people are knee-deep in FUD." Sam smiled, awaiting Jennifer's question.

"Okay, I give up. What's FUD?"

"It's an acronym I coined for three feelings that drag people down in uncertain times: fear, uncertainty, and doubt: FUD. It's just like it sounds—gloomy, thick, sticky, dead weight, no movement."

"FUD—that's a perfect description of how I've been feeling the last couple of days—very fuddy." Jennifer managed to squeeze out a chuckle.

"Listen to me, Jen. Your mental game is the base from which you operate. It affects everything you do and plan to do. Whatever

Your mentality

is your reality!

➤

your mental state, you can be sure your actions and results will reflect it. Your mentality is your reality!"

"I hear you, Sam, but with Neil out of commission, all that FUD out there, and Needleman breathing down my neck, I'm having a hard time thinking positive."

"Getting control of your mental game is a lot more than just thinking positively," said Sam. "It's about assuming control of, and responsibility for, your game. You control your thoughts, motivation, mood, and actions. You are the one driving your bus, not the economy, not Needleman, not the media, not anyone or anything outside of yourself. It is all you. You create your world. You cause it all. This is called **being at-cause**."

"But I didn't cause this tough market. And it's real, regardless of my state of mind!"

Sam continued, "Yes, it is. That's the current set of conditions. There are always conditions or circumstances—sometimes they seem favorable, and other times, not so favorable. Being at-cause is about adjusting your focus, constantly bringing it back to the outcomes you want, regardless of the circumstances.

Being at-cause is about adjusting your focus, constantly bringing it back to the outcomes you want, regardless of the circumstances.

"On the other hand, when you blame the circumstances or someone or something else for your situation—like you've done lately—you are **being at-effect**. And when you're at-effect, you attract the very things you **don't** want."

"I know this stuff, Sam. I read *Sell the Feeling.*"

"It's great that you know it, but what are you doing with this knowledge? When you get caught up in the societal trance and let your thoughts and emotions carry you away, are you being at-cause or at-effect?"

"I guess I am being at-effect, but what can I do about it?"

"You can start by going on a diet," said Sam, bluntly.

Jennifer was taken aback. She was in good physical shape and worked hard to stay that way.

"Pardon me?"

Sam shot back, "Stop taking in all that junk! I'm talking about a **media diet**. You are the gatekeeper of your mind—be at-cause for what you take in. Get the facts you need to stay informed, then tune out or turn off the media if it doesn't support you."

"I can do that, Sam, but Neil likes to watch cable news. Oops, there I go, being at-effect. I suppose I can always go into another room, or ask him to."

Sam was hot about this topic, "Sometimes I refer to the media as the Evil Hypnotist. Don't let the Evil Hypnotist put you into a negative trance. Feed your mind with things that support you. Here's the larger point: be at-cause for your own attitudes, actions, and results."

Jennifer replied, "Sell the Felling 101, right?"

"Right. Now, tell me about your so-called three strikes."

Jennifer told Sam about the icy blow-off she received from Rita Rauche, the bank VP who said she was too busy to refer Jennifer.

"You didn't ask her the state-evoker question," said Sam. "Why not?"

"Rita is a high-level, no-nonsense person. I just couldn't do the touchy-feely thing with her. I think I was a little afraid of looking needy. Plus, I just couldn't bear the thought of asking what she thought of me and maybe getting rejected."

Sam raised his palms into the 'stop' position, saying, "Whoa! Where did you get the idea that asking, 'What are some of the things that have worked for you in our working together?' is equivalent to asking her what she thinks of you? It's not about fishing for compliments. The state-evoker question is a suggestion for your client to go into a state that will allow her to consider whom she can help by referring you."

"You're right, Sam."

"It's not about **me** being right. It's about **your** Ugly Sisters. You just raised two of them: the fear of appearing needy and the fear of rejection.

"Jen, your state of desperation is distracting you from the value of your work and service to others. Because your business is off, you may feel needy at this particular point in time. Regardless of how you feel, remember that you have provided great service, and that if your client is in a state of appreciation, she will probably be more than happy to refer you. I suggest you stop branding yourself as needy. Like Neil said, 'Shut up, focus up, and do the work!'"

"I hear you, Sam, but this fear of rejection is on my mind a lot. Neil said I should talk with you about it."

"Tell me more about it."

"I know it doesn't make sense. After all, I've been a professional salesperson for years. But I still have this nagging fear of being rejected. When Rita said she couldn't think of any referrals for me, I felt completely blown off. I was angry and had a gnawing feeling in the pit of my stomach.

"It made me think of something that happened when I was in high school," she said. "Back in 10th grade, I had a crush on Tommy Nelson. We had this thing called the Sadie Hawkins dance where the girls asked boys for dates. I wanted to ask Tommy, but I was scared, so I waited until the day before the dance to ask him. When I finally got up the courage to ask, he already had a date. He was very sweet about it, but I felt humiliated. I wound up staying home and getting sick from beer I snuck out of the basement refrigerator."

"Did you ever get together with Tommy after that?"

"Nope. I avoided him like the plague for the rest of the year. Even if he had wanted to ask me out, I am sure I put him off. When I saw him, I always went the opposite direction. I know it sounds silly, but as I tell you this story, I still feel it."

"That's the power of Instant Recall[2]—only you're using it to recall a negative state, rather than a positive one. It sounds like you rejected yourself every step of the way."

---

2 Described in *Sell the Feeling* by Larry Pinci and Phil Glosserman.

"How did I reject myself?"

"Because you were afraid, you intentionally waited until the last minute to ask Tommy out, which decreased your odds of getting the date. That was self-rejection. When you finally did ask, he told you he was already committed, but you chose to take it personally. That was self-rejection. And after that, you chose to feel humiliated and avoid him, even though you liked him and he had never done anything to discourage you. That was self-rejection. And the way you are talking about it today, it sounds like you are still carrying around that feeling of rejection. There's a whole lot of self-rejection going on."

"I guess you've got my number, Sam."

"Yours and a lot of other people's. I can't tell you how much unnecessary suffering is caused by the fear of rejection. Because of this irrational fear, many professionals procrastinate or even freeze up on certain activities that would almost certainly bring in more business. It's a shame, because rejection is almost always self-generated, self-contained, and without any basis in reality."

Sam continued, "Eleanor Roosevelt once said, 'No one can make you feel inferior without your consent.' I say no one can make you feel rejected, except you!"

"Sam, you hit the nail on the head with what I went through with Tommy. But what about the current situation? Rita actually said she couldn't think of anyone, and she didn't give me a referral. She rejected my request, right? I know this is a weird question, but aren't I entitled to feel rejected?"

No one can make you feel rejected, except you!

→

"You're entitled to feel however you want, but why put yourself through needless anxiety? Someone may not be able to refer you right now, but how is that a rejection of **you**? Rita told you she was too preoccupied to think about referring you now. But instead of accepting what she told you at face value, or instead of questioning whether you left something out of your process, you interpreted her response as a rejection of **you**. Isn't that a little self-centered?

the referral code

"At the very least you could have opened the possibility to have a referral conversation in the future, by saying 'Not a problem. We can revisit this next time we get together.'"

Jennifer grimaced.

Sam said, "I bet you're beating yourself up on the inside, aren't you?"

Nervously chuckling, she replied, "What are you, a mind-reader?"

"Once again, Jen, this is about getting beyond yourself. Instead of obsessing about what you did or didn't do in the past, you could be thinking about the possibilities you can open up and what you will do now."

"Sam I hear you, but I have one question about what I did in the past: Do you think I blew it with Rita by not asking the state-evoker question?"

"If you're asking whether I think the results would have been different if you had gotten her into a state of appreciation, the answer is—most likely. But like I said, keep looking forward. You can always go back to Rita when you're ready.

"Your experience with Rita raises an important point: **Never ask for referrals outside of a state of appreciation.** Remember the story of my granddaughter asking for cookies after her parents praised her for cleaning up her room? Imagine if she had asked while they were cleaning up a flood in the kitchen."

Never ask for referrals outside of a state of appreciation.

"Okay, I get the point, Sam."

"Good. I don't think your call with her was a strike. She said she didn't have time to think about referring you and that if she came up with any ideas, she would let you know. You can go back to her at another time.

"I want you to get this into your bones. It will undoubtedly come up again in one form or another. Someone may not think of referrals for you the first or second time you ask, but she may come up with a home-run referral the third or fourth time. Or a prospect may not be ready to do business with you right now, but he may be ready in six months or a year. Keep these people on your list and keep following up. Always remember that delays are not denials."

"That's great advice, Sam. Like a lot of producers I know, I focus so much on the deals at-hand that I neglect almost anything that seems like it won't bear fruit immediately."

Delays are not denials.

Sam responded, "I call that **deal blindness**. It's when you can't see opportunities that could bring you future returns because you're so immersed in present deals."

"You're right, Sam. I'm beginning to see the light at the end of the tunnel."

Sam quipped, "And it's definitely not an oncoming train!"

They laughed together.

Jennifer continued, "Okay, Sam. I'll cycle back with Rita at a later date, and I'll keep a running list of people to continue following up with."

Deal blindness is when you can't see opportunities that could bring you future returns because you're so immersed in present deals.

"Good, Jen. Now tell me about the other two referral conversations."

Jennifer told him about her call to Rick Hancock, the COO who was no longer at the company.

Sam asked, "Do you know why he's no longer there?"

"I assume he was laid off."

"How come?"

Jennifer answered curtly, "Because the economy has wrecked so many businesses, Sam. I just naturally assumed he was canned. He must be devastated, and it would be insensitive and brash for me to call at this particular moment to ask him for referrals."

"Another Ugly Sister—you don't want to come off as pushy. Jen, you don't know that he was laid off. He may have left voluntarily for another position, or because he won the lottery, or to take a sabbatical. And even if he were laid off, he may be okay with it. You don't know—you assumed. To unlock a constant stream of business through the power of your relationships, you have got to get beyond your false assumptions and limiting beliefs."

> *To unlock a constant stream of business through the power of your relationships, you have got to get beyond your false assumptions and limiting beliefs.*
>
> ➜

"Honestly, Sam. I was thinking of **him**."

"I can appreciate that. Do you have any way of getting in touch with him?"

"I have his cell phone number."

"Then I suggest you call him and check in to see how he is. If he did get laid off, wish him well and see if you can do anything to help. Once you understand his situation, you can decide whether to have the referral conversation. The larger point is this: you're playing the referral game too tentatively—too deferentially."

"Okay. You are absolutely right. I'll call him tomorrow."

"Good. Now tell me about your third conversation."

Jennifer told Sam about Nancy Hellman at the temp agency.

"I truly wanted to have the referral conversation with her," said Jennifer. "She's one of my best clients and a huge fan. As we were talking, she even told me they loved our work and planned to renew their contract with us. It seemed like she was in a naturally occurring state of appreciation, but she was stressed over her budget meetings and kept talking about the economic slowdown and cutbacks. It just didn't seem like the right time to ask."

Teeing-Up a Referral When the Timing Isn't Right to Ask

"Jen, it's good that you paid attention to your instincts. There may be times when your client is in a state of appreciation, but the timing doesn't seem quite right for the referral conversation. This is a perfect example—Nancy was in a state of appreciation, but you sensed she was too distracted by her budget woes to give you her full attention.

"Another example might be if your client is in a state of appreciation but is in a rush to get somewhere, or other people are present who might interfere with the conversation. In these instances, it's a good idea to capture the state and plant the seeds for a future referral conversation. I call it the **referral conversation tee-up**."

"Sounds interesting, Sam. How do I do it?"

Sam continued, "Let's take the case with Nancy, who was in a naturally occurring state of appreciation about you and your work. You could have said, 'Thanks for positive feedback, Nancy. When you finish this run of budget meetings, I'd like to talk with you about who you know that could benefit from the same kind of service you've experienced with us and have been so happy with. Why don't we connect on that in a couple of weeks.'

"If you are doing this in-person, I suggest you nod your head as you make the suggestion about connecting in a couple of weeks. When you nod, people will often nod along with you. When someone nods with you, it implants the suggestion deeper."

"What's the purpose of prepping her like that?"

"You're planting a suggestion in her unconscious mind to remember the state of appreciation and to be thinking about who she can refer."

Sam continued, "When you cycle back with Nancy, you can remind her of your previous conversation by saying, 'Nancy, remember when we last spoke and you told me how much you appreciate our service?' That will trigger an emotional memory of her state of appreciation. Then you can go ahead and ask her the referral question: 'I was wondering, who do you know…'"

"I like this tee-up, Sam. I'm sure I can use it."

Sam added, "The tee-up has some important elements. Be sure to use the person's name and give a timeframe for getting back to him or her. Then say, 'I would like to talk with you about who you know that can benefit from the responsiveness, cost-effectiveness, or whatever the person appreciates about your service.

"Imagine that you're at a business dinner with a number of other people, and your client, Bonnie, expresses appreciation for the great service you've provided. Normally, you don't want to launch into the full-blown referral conversation when other people are present. Instead, at an appropriate moment, you would do the tee-up. How would you say it?"

Jennifer replied, "Bonnie, in the next couple of weeks, I'd like to talk with you about who you know that can benefit from the same kind of great service you said we've provided."

"Perfect!" Sam exclaimed. "The great thing about the tee-up is that it gives the other person two options. They can have the referral conversation with you later, or they might start volunteering referrals right then and there.

"One more thing, Jen. Remember the timeframe—keep your word and cycle back within the time you specified. I suggest making it no more than a month. You don't want the memory to become too distant."

"Sounds good, Sam. So what's next?"

"I have an assignment for you. Next time we get together, I'm going to show you how to lay out your plan to get referrals using something I call the Referral Matrix. To prepare, I want you to go through your database, business cards, address book, and memory and list up to 20 people that love you and may be connected with people who match your referral type. Think about these six categories."

1. clients, current and past from current and past jobs

2. partners, associates, and vendors

3. business network

4. memberships and affiliations

5. family and friends

6. other professionals

"Remember," said Sam, "you're looking for people who love you and the work you do, that have people they love that love them too, who need to love you."

Jennifer responded, "I don't get how family and friends figure into this. They may love me, but they don't have a direct experience of my work."

"We'll get to that at another meeting. For now, just compile the list. The important thing is that you pick people that love you—or who think highly of you—and are likely to be connected into relationships that match your referral type.

"One more thing: As you go through your database, look for anyone who might be a natural connector or promoter—someone who loves to connect people or promote ideas, causes, or people they believe in."

"I know what you mean, Sam. Actually, my friend Rose fits that description. She has a PR company and she knows people all over the country. Any time Rose is hot on something, she sends out emails to everyone she knows."

"Perfect. Put Rose on the list."

"Before you leave, Jen, there's something I need to talk with you about. I just got a call from a dear friend of mine who invited me on the trip of a lifetime. I'm going to be gone and incommunicado for the next four weeks. Sorry to spring this on you at the last minute, but I just found out."

"That sounds exciting, Sam. What kind of trip?"

"It's an extended rafting trip down the Colorado River through the Grand Canyon. My friend booked this trip years ago for a group of his friends. He called me last night to ask me if I wanted to take the place of someone who had to drop out at the last minute. This trip is supposed to be incredible. It's a dream-come-true for me."

"Wow that sounds great, Sam."

"I'm sorry to have to interrupt our meetings. You have some work to do before I get back. You can still focus on your top five clients, including going back to bat with the three we talked about today. Go ahead and put together the list of people we talked about, but I suggest you hold off on contacting them until we have a chance to go over it. I need to show you how to pace your game."

"I'll miss our meetings, Sam, but of course I understand. I hope you have a great trip—it sounds wonderful!"

"Thanks, Jen. What do you take away from this meeting?"

"I need to stop throwing myself into a tizzy over what's going on in the economy and the market. I'm going to take your advice and tune out the media when it doesn't support me. The bottom line is that I'm at-cause for my thoughts and actions. You helped me get back on track. I'm committed to being at-cause."

"Jen, it's important that you monitor yourself. If you find yourself lagging, blaming others, feeling rejected, or blaming circumstances, notice that you are being at-effect. Remind yourself of your commitment to be at-cause."

"Will do, Sam. I've seen the light!"

"Hallelujah!" Sam chuckled.

As Sam walked Jennifer to the door, he gave her a squeeze on the shoulder and said, "I know you'll integrate everything we've talked about so far and generate some great referrals by the time I get back. I'll see you in a month."

As Jennifer walked to her car, she felt that she had thrown off the worries and negativity that had been stifling her. She looked forward to launching into the next phase of the Referral Code, but she felt a little anxious about not being able to talk with Sam for such a long time.

I wonder if I can keep my attitude in check for a whole month, thought Jen. Then she remembered what Sam had said about getting beyond herself. She renewed her commitment to be at-cause for her attitude, actions, and results.

back at bat

the next morning, Jennifer called Rick Hancock on his cell phone.

"Hi, Rick. It's Jennifer Stewart. I tried calling your office, but the receptionist said you were no longer working there. I wanted to check in to see how you're doing."

"Thanks so much for calling, Jennifer. I'm just fine, and I'm glad to hear from you. I had you on my list to call this week, but you beat me to it. The company is going through some restructuring and layoffs. Frankly, I disagreed with a number of things about the direction the company is moving in. They offered me a severance package, and I took it, gladly."

Jennifer responded, "You sound pretty good, all things considered. I hope you'll find something that fits what you're looking for."

"I'll be fine. I already have some potential opportunities lined up."

Rick and Jennifer continued catching up for the next several minutes, then Rick added, "I wanted to call you this week to suggest you contact the CFO, Anne Marsh. She will be your new contact for the time being. I told her what an outstanding job you and your team have done. You guys pulled us through some difficult technical challenges. I highly recommended that they renew your service agreement when it comes up later this year."

Jennifer could tell that Rick was in a naturally occurring state of appreciation, so the time felt right to have the referral conversation.

"Thanks so much, Rick. I'll call Anne this week. "As long as I have you on the phone, I was wondering, who do you know that can benefit from the same outstanding service you just described—an organization with at least two hundred people that may have technical challenges like your company did?"

"Let me think," said Rick, pausing for a moment. "Have you ever spoken with Randstat Logistics—the defense contractor? A good buddy of mine is the CEO. I'd be happy to call him on your behalf."

"That would be great, Rick."

"Also, I'm still good friends with my old college roommate, Joe Hicks. He owns a company that distributes food to restaurants. They're growing like gangbusters. I know they are dealing with all sorts of challenges related to their IT infrastructure. I owe Joe a call. I'll talk to him about you."

"Thanks, Rick. I really appreciate…"

"Oh, you've got me thinking. There's one more: my father-in-law is one of the founding partners of a large law firm that has offices in eight cities. I'm seeing him tonight. And I'll be sure to put in a word for you wherever I land. I'll let you know if I think of anyone else in the meantime."

"Thanks so much, Rick. You know one of the things I appreciate about working with you is the way you always come up with creative possibilities," *especially in this call,* she thought.

Jennifer finished the referral conversation by getting the necessary contact information and promising Rick she would follow up with him in a week or so. Needless to say, she was overwhelmed by his positive response. After all she had been through in the past few months, she wished she could reach through the phone and hug him.

"Good talking to you, Rick," she said. "Please let me know if I can do anything for you."

For the first time in weeks, Jennifer felt a rush of positive energy. It made her realize how down she had been. She was now charged-up and ready for action. She realized that Rick must be a natural promoter, like Sam talked about.

In her energized state, Jennifer wasted no time in hatching plans for re-approaching Nancy, the IT director who was stressed over budget meetings, and Rita Rauche who had given her the 'icy blow-off.'

She decided to call Nancy and invite her to lunch once she finished the current round of budget meetings.

"Why thanks, Jennifer," Nancy said when Jennifer called. "That would be great. Let's put something on the calendar for next week."

Good. Now that I've got lunch with Nancy set up, what should I do with Rita? This is a tough one. I helped make her a star at her bank and she knows it, but she told me she didn't have time to even think about referring me.

Suddenly, she felt a gnawing feeling in the pit of her stomach. She quickly identified it as the fear of being seen as pushy, needy, and of being rejected.

A triple whammy—all Three Ugly Sisters at once! She laughed out loud at herself. *Well, at least I'm not taking myself so seriously.*

I wonder what Sam would advise me to do? I wish I could call him, but he's probably somewhere in the middle of the Grand Canyon. Okay, think—there must be a good way to do this. Rita is a great client. She has always been friendly, and she has told me on more than one occasion how much she valued what we did for her. Maybe I just caught her at a bad time. Things could be different if I approached her at a different time. I should invite her to have coffee and find out more about how her operations are going and what initiatives they may be planning in the future. I'll feel her out. If the timing doesn't seem right to ask for referrals again, I'll just wait until another time.

She called Rita and invited her to have coffee in two weeks. Rita seemed more relaxed and welcomed the chance to get out of the office and meet with her.

The following week, Jennifer called Rick Hancock to follow up.

Rick told Jennifer, "I put in calls to all the people we talked about. The defense contracting company is a no-go. They handle their entire IT operations in-house—they're required to do so by government regulations. I talked to my father-in-law, and his firm is very happy with their current IT provider.

"But I do have some good new for you," said Rick. "I just got off the phone with Joe Hicks, my college roommate who owns the food distribution company. He suggested you talk to his IT director. I gave him your number, and he said he would pass it on."

"Thanks so much, Rick. I'll wait to hear from him and let you know what happens."

Jennifer was a bit disappointed. She had been excited about Rick's three potential referrals, and now she only had one guy who might call her sometime. She was relying on Rick's friend Joe to suggest to his IT director to call her. She hadn't asked Rick for the IT director's contact info because it sounded like Rick didn't even know his name. She felt she had lost control of the game with this referral. For the moment, she was resigned to wait for the IT director's call.

That same week, Jennifer met Nancy Hellman for lunch. Done with her budget meetings, Nancy seemed much more at-ease. Jennifer spent some time finding out what was happening in Nancy's world. Then she asked the state-evoker question.

"Nancy, what are some of the things that have worked for you in our working together?"

"It's been really good working with you," said Nancy. "Everyone on your service team has been responsive and knowledgeable. I think what stands out for me is the cost savings. You guys came in close to 20 percent below the other bids we received and the service has been uniformly excellent."

"Thanks, Nancy. I was wondering…" Jennifer paused for a moment, as if contemplating what to say next. "Who do you know that can benefit from the same kind of excellent service and cost savings you described—a company with two hundred or more employees?"

"Oh, Jennifer, I'd be happy to refer you, but I need some time to think. Can I get back to you on this?"

"No problem. Why don't I go ahead and follow up with you in a week or so to see who has come to mind."

The next week, Jennifer called Nancy.

"Oh, Jennifer. I'm sorry. I haven't had a chance to look into it. I promise I will."

"No problem. Why don't I follow up with you in a week or so."

When she followed up the next week, Nancy said she was embarrassed, but she still hadn't looked into it.

"I'm so sorry," Nancy said when Jennifer followed up the next week. "I just can't think of anyone that meets your criteria for two hundred people. I wish I had someone for you. I will keep my eyes and ears open and let you know—I promise."

Jennifer got off the phone and thought, *Normally I'd take this as a rejection, but I'm not playing that game anymore. I gave it my best shot with Nancy and I'll take her at her word. Maybe she'll have someone for me later. Next!*

As she drove up to the restaurant, Jennifer was slightly nervous about her lunch with Rita Rauche. She reminded herself of the value she and her company had brought to Rita and her bank. She also remembered how appreciative Rita had been in the past. She remembered her commitment to be at-cause and that she would no longer interpret resistance or delays as signs of rejection.

At lunch, Rita seemed much less stressed than the last time they met. She and Jennifer chatted for a bit about business and other common interests.

At one point Rita said, "Jennifer, I believe I may have been a bit curt with you last time we met. I'm glad you called me for lunch, because it gives me a chance to apologize. I know you wanted to talk to me about something. I'm sorry if I cut you off."

"Thanks, Rita. No problem. I just wanted to talk to you a bit about our service. I was wondering what are some of the things that have worked for you in our working together?"

"I'll tell you Jennifer, you guys have had a significant positive impact on our IT functioning." Rita spent the next couple of minutes describing several benefits of the infrastructure changes and finished up by saying, "The bottom line is that the initiatives you brought have improved our efficiency and throughput in a big way. We are more than satisfied."

"Thanks so much, Rita. I was wondering, who do you know that can benefit from some of the same kinds of services you described that improved your efficiency and throughput—a company with at least two hundred employees?"

"Good question. No one comes to mind this instant, but let me think it over, okay?"

Jennifer responded, "No problem. Why don't I go ahead and give you a call in a week or so and see who has come to mind?"

"That would be fine, Jennifer."

When Jen got into her car to leave, she reached over her shoulder and physically gave herself a pat on the back.

Good recovery. Let's see what happens, she told herself.

When she got back to the office, Jennifer was pleasantly surprised to hear a voicemail from Rick Hancock.

"I thought of someone else for you," Rick's message said. "His name is Mark Mitchell, and he is the CEO of a national document storage company. He's interested in talking with you. Give me a call when you get this, and I'll give you the details."

Jennifer called Rick, who told her that Mark wanted her to call him at the end of the week.

"That's great Rick. Thanks so much. I'll call him Friday

Jennifer decided to gain control of the referral to the IT director at the food distribution company.

"Rick, as long as I've got you on the line, I haven't heard from the food distributor you told me about. I was wondering if there's any way you can get me contact info for the IT director."

"I think that's a good idea, Jennifer. Sometimes these guys get so busy—you know how it is. I'll send the CEO an email and get back to you."

That afternoon, Jennifer received an email from Rick with the IT director's name and telephone number.

By the end of the week, she had called Rick's referrals and scheduled meetings with both of them. Before she went home for the weekend, she surveyed her week's results:

```
79 cold calls, 14 actual contacts, 1 follow-up phone
introductory meeting scheduled

3 referral conversations, 2 referrals, (more coming,
possibly), 2 meetings scheduled
```

It was blindingly obvious where her time and energy were better spent.

the L-word

The following Tuesday, Jennifer got a call from Rick Hancock, "I just wanted you to know that last weekend I saw Mark from the document storage company. I sang your praises. He told me you're meeting this week. Good luck."

"That's great, Rick. Thanks so much."

"And by the way, I'm closing in on an opportunity to become regional VP of a financial services company. One of the mandates of the job is to bring their IT infrastructure into the 21st century. If I get this job, I will see to it that you get in the door."

"Thanks for your support, Rick. I look forward to the opportunity. Good luck on the job offer."

Jennifer met with both of Rick's referrals that week. Before doing so, she reviewed *Sell the Feeling* to ground herself in her selling conversation.

The meeting with the IT director of the food services company went well. He agreed to the next step: Jennifer would send in a rep from her engineering team to perform a technical needs analysis, after which they would do a full-scale proposal.

She also met with Mark Mitchell from the document storage company. He was mostly satisfied with his current service provider, but he had agreed to meet with Jennifer on the strength of Rick's recommendation. By the time Jennifer had sold him the feeling, he also agreed to a technical needs analysis.

Jennifer was feeling absolutely great.

the referral code

And then she heard her coworker Laura mention 'the L-word.'

"Layoffs!" Jennifer exclaimed. "In the sales department? You have got to be kidding! I know we're struggling, but the sales department is the last place that should face cutbacks. Where did you hear this, Laura?"

"Needleman's assistant overheard him talking on the phone with the CEO. He said something about a 30 percent reduction across all departments."

Jennifer went back to the office and tried to analyze her chances of being cut. She had been at PITS for a little over a year and was viewed by many as a rising star. Her actual sales performance put her smack dab in the middle of the department. Unfortunately, her book of business, which had declined significantly since the economy had started to tumble, was in the bottom third of her department.

Needleman was a former military man who believed in command and control. He wanted things done his way, and Jennifer was sure that he was somewhat irked by her independent spirit. Unlike some others in her department, she had not sucked up to him, and her cold calling had produced no sales. She was not making Needleman look good.

And another thing concerned her: During the past two weeks, she had not met Needleman's minimum requirements on her cold-calling numbers. Despite the fact that she had two positive meetings from referrals, she knew Needleman was scrutinizing her numbers and would not be pleased.

Jennifer thought, *My head could definitely be on the chopping block. I may need to do some damage control with Needlenose. I'd like to talk it over with Neil, but he's got that damn contraption on his jaw. I need more advice than he can give me on that stupid blackboard. I wish I could talk with Sam, but he's not due back for another two weeks.*

Jennifer left the office, her head spinning and imagining the worst. Her stomach tightened into a knot and she felt that unsettling combination of uncertainty and dread that is all-too-familiar to anyone who has ever worked at a company threatened by layoffs.

don't tell him, *sell* him

When Jennifer got home, Neil snuck up and gave her a hug from behind. Startled, she turned around, and Neil planted a big kiss on her lips—the first one in months.

"Honey! Oh my God. Where's your contraption?"

"The doctor took it off today, a couple weeks earlier than I expected."

They spent the next half an hour celebrating with champagne and more kisses. Then Jennifer told Neil about the layoff rumor and her concerns.

"Do you think I should go to Needleman and tell him about how I'm generating referrals?"

"Maybe. What outcome are you after?"

"I want to keep my job and see this whole referral process through."

"Is that all?

"You know what I really want, Neil? I want to quit wasting so much of my valuable time trying to make cold-calling numbers just to keep Needleman off my back."

"What would you do with your valuable time instead?"

"You know that Sam asked me to come up with a list of people to ask for referrals, right? I want to focus my time on those people. I'm convinced that's my best shot for creating new business—not calling on people that don't know me from Adam and who are hanging onto their shorts in a market downturn."

Neil replied, "You know what I think? You should convince Needleman to let you do what you really want. What have you got to lose?"

"You mean tell him I want to quit cold calling so I can concentrate on referrals?"

"No. I don't mean **tell** him—**sell** him. Show him that your successfully implementing the referral strategy is in **his best interest and the company's best interest**. You believe you will generate better results through referrals than by cold calling, don't you?"

"Of course, I do."

"Then why don't you go ahead and propose to Needleman that you spend your time generating referrals, and if you don't hit some minimum standard of success in a certain timeframe, you'll go back to cold calling."

"How do I do that? He's stuck on cold calling like white on rice."

"Find out what's really important to him," Neil gave Jennifer a knowing look.

Jennifer thought about it for a few moments, then the light went on in her eyes. "I get it—you mean sell him the feeling!"

"Yep."

"Now **that's** an intriguing idea! Thanks, Neil. You got that contraption off just in time."

roger comes around

On Sunday afternoon, Jennifer reviewed the steps of *Sell the Feeling* and planned her strategy with Needleman.[3]

Step 1: Prepare

First, Jennifer decided on her closing point—the outcome she wanted from her meeting with Needleman. She wanted two months to concentrate on her referrals without being distracted by cold calling. She would measure her success by the number of new companies that agreed to a meeting.

Jennifer anticipated that Needleman would be reluctant to let her focus on referral conversations while holding the rest of the department to the 90-calls-per-week requirement. She came up with a proposal that just might work. She could use her 60 days as a pilot project. If she demonstrated positive results, she would offer to teach the Referral Code to her colleagues. Knowing Needleman's ego, she would have to propose this in a way that could make him look like a hero.

Next, she profiled Needleman. She already knew a lot about him, but she decided to look him up on the Web to see if she could find any information that might help. After about 20 minutes of sifting through various articles, she found exactly what she needed: an old interview with Needleman from an industry trade journal. The interviewer asked him about his sales management philosophy. Needleman was quoted as saying:

---

3 The steps described in this chapter are from *Sell the Feeling: The 6-Step System that Drives People to Do Business with You* by Larry Pinci and Phil Glosserman.

"The bottom line is: the numbers don't lie. Over the last 10 years, we have employed various strategies to penetrate new markets. Depending on the situation—the current economy, the competitive landscape, and other factors—sometimes you have to look at what is working and what is not and make a conscious decision to shift gears. You have to look carefully at your numbers on a regular basis and adjust your sales and marketing strategies accordingly. That's a tough call for some managers because they don't want to risk leaving the impression that what they have been doing all along has been ineffective. Sometimes you can't know for sure how a new strategy will play out until you actually go for it. And there are strategies that only work for a season. When you shift strategies, you may wind up with egg on your face, but on the other hand, you may get your biggest win."

Jennifer decided that if the opportunity presented itself, she would use Needleman's own words to make her case. This could be tricky. If Needleman realized she was using his words from an old interview to influence him, he might feel that she was being underhanded and reject her proposal outright.

Next, she decided on the state she needed to be in: a state of self-confidence. She also decided what feelings she wanted to create with Needleman: trust, confidence, and a feeling of being respected.

Monday morning, she called Needleman's assistant and arranged a meeting for that afternoon. Just before heading to his office, she reminded herself of her closing point and visualized a successful meeting in which Needleman agreed to her proposal. Then she used Instant Recall[4] to put herself into a state of confidence and reminded herself of the feelings she wanted to evoke in Needleman: trust, confidence, and respect.

---

4 Described in *Sell the Feeling*.

Step 2: Create Rapport

Jennifer entered Needleman's office and sat down. They exchanged pleasantries and engaged in some small talk. As they talked, Jennifer matched and mirrored Roger. When he leaned forward, she subtly and unobtrusively leaned forward. When he put his hands on his desk with his fingers interlaced, she did the same. She also matched his pace of speech. Needleman spoke more slowly than Jennifer, so she adjusted her pace to his. After a couple minutes of matching and mirroring, Jennifer began to notice a feeling of connectedness.

Once she felt rapport, Jennifer explained the reason for her visit, "Roger, I want to talk with you about some of the things I've been doing to generate more leads."

Roger responded, "I see you've scheduled two new technical analyses. Way to go. Your cold calling is finally paying off."

Jennifer resisted her temptation to tell Needleman that cold calling had produced virtually nothing for her. She knew that insinuating Roger was wrong in any way would hurt her chances of success. She reminded herself to maintain rapport and continued matching and mirroring him.

She replied, "Yes, things are starting to turn around."

Step 3: Ask Questions

The next step was to ask questions. Jennifer knew that one of the main keys to a successful outcome was to elicit and address Needleman's emotional needs. She moved straight to the emotional needs question: What's important to you about x?

"Roger, I've been employing some additional strategies to get new leads. Before I run them by you, I was wondering, what's important to you about a lead-generation program that really works?"

Roger didn't hesitate, "Three things. First, I want to measure activity on an ongoing basis. Second, I want every rep to have a definite game plan and execute it. In my 20-plus years of managing salespeople, I've seen far too many reps waste time day after day. Third, I want quantifiable results. If someone is hitting their call numbers and not turning contacts into meetings, there's no point, is there? I expect my reps to generate at least four prospect meetings a month."

"I agree, Roger. What else is important to you about a lead-generation program?"

"It's got to be systematic and reproducible. Everyone gets lucky once in awhile, but luck is not a strategy for business success. I want people coming to work, knowing what they need to do to get leads and turn them into business."

While Roger was talking, Jennifer jotted down his emotional needs in his words.

Step 4: Link

The next step was to link Needleman's needs with her proposal.

"Great, Roger. If I could show you a lead-generation system that is systematic and reproducible, includes measurable activity and a definite game plan, and by using it, I meet or exceed four meetings a month, would you be interested in learning more about it?"

"You've got my attention. If it does everything you say and you can meet or exceed your quota, I'd like to hear about it. But this is all very theoretical. What kind of lead system are you talking about?"

Jennifer told Roger about her work with Sam and her results so far with the Referral Code. Now that she had his interest, she felt she could tell him the source of her recent success.

"Roger, I've got a confession: the two technical analysis sessions I set up are a direct result of the referrals I've been working."

"This is all quite intriguing," said Roger. "I must commend you for the activity you're generating."

Step 5: Close

Needleman was coming around. He was showing interest and seemed to be open to suggestion. Jennifer sensed that it was time to get to the offer and close him.

"Roger, let me get to the point. I know you want me to succeed, and I want to help you and the company succeed. In the three weeks since I started implementing the Referral Code system, I've had meetings with three new potential accounts and signed up two of them to do a technical analysis. I've researched these companies, and they are all potentially big accounts for us. In two months of cold calling, I've scheduled a couple of meetings, but they've been dead-ends. For some reason, cold calling is not working for me, but the Referral Code is.

"This business of getting and working referrals is a lot of work. If I had the time, Roger, I could do so much more with the relationships I already have. I've created a lot of goodwill with my clients and associates. I know I can turn that goodwill into business, but I need the time to do it. I just can't maximize **our** success if I have to make 90 calls a week."

Needleman interrupted, "Jennifer, I get what you're saying, and I see that this Referral Code, as you call it, is working for you. But I can't make you an exception to my cold-calling mandate. The rest of the sales team would be pounding on my door wanting exceptions of their own. That's no way to run a company."

"I can appreciate your concern, Roger," said Jennifer, remembering to acknowledge the objection before handling it. "If I were in your position, I'd be hesitant to have one maverick salesperson off doing her own thing."

Jennifer continued, "I'd like to open up a different perspective. I've looked at the sales reports, and I can see we're down almost 40 percent from this time last year."

Roger blew out a breath between his pursed lips, acknowledging the hard facts and whispered, "Yep."

the referral code

Now was as good a time as any to use Needleman's words from the interview she found on the Web, "Roger, I know times are tough, but you know as well as I do that the numbers don't lie. Sometimes you have to look at what's working and what's not and make a conscious decision to change gears, or at least try something different."

As she echoed Needleman's words, she noticed his eyes glisten and his head nodding slightly.

"What if you were to authorize me to conduct a short pilot project?" Remembering Needleman's military history, she added, "A secret operation—a kind of skunk works."

"Go on," said Needleman his eyes opening a bit wider.

"Give me 60 days," said Jennifer. Remembering that Needleman loved competition, she improvised, "Put me up against anyone in the department. If I can prove to you—if I can show you that I can generate more qualified leads that turn into meetings than anyone doing cold calling—I will follow it up with a proposal to teach this system to the rest of the sales team under your supervision. All I'm asking is 60 days. If I produce, we all win. If not, I will go back to cold calling. It will be our secret. What have you got to lose?"

Roger interlaced his fingers and peered across his desk at Jennifer without speaking. She waited for his response. A few seconds later, she matched him, slowly interlacing her fingers.

Finally, Roger spoke, measuring his words carefully, "I admire your initiative, Jennifer. If I agree to this, and you deliver good results, your program may be worth further inspection. But I must tell you—and this is between the two of us—at this critical juncture in our business, the company is scrutinizing performance across all areas. The CEO is a strong advocate for my cold-calling program and wants me to enforce it strictly. Your proposition is not without personal risk."

Jennifer read Needleman's message loud and clear. If she didn't deliver, she'd be out the door. In the current economy, it was not a good time to be out on the streets looking for a job. On the other hand, she couldn't bear the thought of any more cold calls.

She decided to go for broke, "I hear you, Roger. I'm still up for the challenge. Sometimes you can't know for sure how a new strategy will play out until you actually go for it. You may wind up with egg on your face, but may get your biggest win."

On hearing Jennifer echo his own words from the 10-year old interview, Roger's face lit up. He didn't realize they were his own words, at least not consciously.

"I like your spirit," he said. "Okay, you can run with your pilot project, but let's keep it strictly between us. I'm going to monitor your progress carefully. I still want a report from you at the end of each week on the number of meetings you've set. If you haven't set at least four meetings by the end of the first 30 days, I reserve the right to reinstate your cold-calling requirements. Understood?"

"Yes, Roger, we're on the same page," she said, silently adding, *for the first time*.

Step 6 – Reassure

Jennifer was delighted. Her strategy had worked like a charm. She had one step to go: have Roger run his reassurance strategy so he would continue to feel good about his decision.

"Roger, I was wondering, what stood out to you in my proposal that convinced you to make this decision today?"

Roger thought for a moment before responding, "It was when you said the numbers don't lie, and it's time to re-evaluate."

Leaning back in his chair with his hands behind his head, he added, "I remember way back when I had my first sales job in Texas. I was 12 at the time. I was part of summer youth program that sold magazines door-to-door. We would wake up early and the program leader would drive us to different neighborhoods so we could knock on doors. By mid-morning, the temperature would be in the 90s.

the referral code

"At the end of each week, the program leader, Mike, had us tally up how many subscriptions we sold. He wrote everyone's numbers up on a blackboard. I usually sold about 12 to 15 a week, which was pretty disappointing. Most of the kids sold about 20 subscriptions a week, and a couple were averaging 40 or 50.

"One day, Mike took me aside and asked why my sales were so consistently low. I told him I was unlucky and that people in my neighborhoods just weren't interested in buying magazines. I remember him pointing to the blackboard and saying, 'It's not luck. Either you're slacking or doing something wrong. These numbers don't lie.'

"The top seller was a kid name Curly Jenkins. Mike paired me up with Curly for a couple of days so I could observe how he sold. Curly was from a poor family. He had several brothers and sisters, and his dad had abandoned the family. I was working because my parents wanted me to do something constructive over the summer. Curly's family really needed the money.

"Curly lived by his wits. When someone answered the door, Curly would smile, introduce himself, then say, 'It's awful hot out today, isn't it?' Then he would pull out his handkerchief, wipe his brow, and say, 'Can I trouble you for a glass of water, ma'am?' Most times, he would be invited into the house. Once inside, he'd talk about the rec center we were building and sweet-talk them into a sale.

"Curly was really clever, and he had a way with people. Your referral strategy reminds me of something he used to do. Once he was done making a sale, he would say, 'I want to thank you so much for supporting our youth group. Do you know any other good people in the neighborhood who might want to help kids in our community the same way as you?' His customers would tell him to go call on that nice Mrs. Smith on Maple Street, or to avoid the old man across the street that didn't like kids.

"After following Curly for a couple days, I changed my approach. I did a lot of the things he did, and guess what? My sales improved. By the end of the summer, I was averaging 24 sales a week: a 100 percent increase over what I was doing before. Like you said, the numbers don't lie."

"Great story, Roger. By the way, thanks for putting your trust in me."

"You bet. Just between us, our cold-calling numbers are way up, but we're not getting the increase in appointments that I had hoped for. Maybe it's time to try something new. I hope you're onto something. I'll be watching. Good luck."

Jennifer left Needleman's office feeling better than she had felt in weeks. Not only did she get what she wanted, but she also created great rapport with him. He had even taken her into his confidence.

As she walked back to her office, she had a thought that stopped her dead in her tracks: *I'm actually starting to like the guy.*

the referral matrix

Jennifer had no time to waste. Sam was due back the next day, and she had not yet finished compiling the list of the people that loved her and her work. She looked at the categories Sam had given her:

1. clients, current and past from current and past jobs

2. partners, associates, and vendors

3. business network

4. memberships and affiliations

5. family and friends

6. other professionals

She also remembered that Sam had asked her to think of anyone who might be a natural promoter or connector.

Jennifer went through her database, business cards, and address book and identified a number of people in each category. She thought about her history with each person and narrowed the list down to 17 people with whom she felt she had created the most goodwill. Just thinking about the goodwill represented in the list gave her a lift. When she included the three people with whom she already had the referral conversation, her total was 20.

One of the people in her Referral Matrix was her good friend and former college roommate, Rose, who owned a PR firm and was president of her local chamber of commerce. Another was her cousin Mitch, a corporate attorney. Neither had experienced her services directly. Because of the nature of their work, she suspected that both had numerous business connections that might match her referral type. She was unsure of how to approach them, or if she would feel comfortable doing so, or if they knew people of her referral type, but Sam assured her that he would show her a way to make it work, so she put them on her list.

The next day, Sam called. Jennifer agreed to meet him the following evening at his home. Sam asked Jennifer to bring her Referral Matrix and her work schedule."

When Jennifer arrived at Sam's house, he greeted her at the door with a warm hug. He was tan and fit from his Colorado River rafting trip.

"How was your trip, Sam?"

"Absolutely incredible! I have lots to tell you, but it will have to wait until another time. Catch me up on what has happened over the past month."

Jennifer told Sam about the leads she had received, and about her new arrangement with Needleman. When she told Sam about selling the feeling to Roger, he broke out in a big smile.

"Brilliant! I'm making you the new poster child for *Sell the Feeling*!"

"Thanks, Sam. I'm actually quite pleased with myself."

"You should be. I am really proud of you. You have 60 days to create what you committed to. Every day counts, so let's get cracking with your Referral Matrix."

Jennifer replied, "I've compiled the list that includes the different categories of people we talked about."

Jennifer laid her list on the table so Sam could look at it. As they went through the list, Jennifer briefly described the people and her relationship with them.

Referral Matrix Categories

CLIENTS (Current & Past)	PARTNERS, ASSOCIATES & VENDORS	BUSINESS NETWORK	FRIENDS & FAMILY	MEMBERSHIPS & AFFILIATIONS	OTHER
Rick Hancock (already called)	Bill Nelson	Al Saunders	Rose Samuelson	Peg Ornstein	Clive Lewis
Rita Rauche (already called)	Jack McGee	Bill Turner	Mitch Hodges	Stephen Simms	
Nancy Hellman (already called)		Pete Walsh		Leighton Wu	
Rob Peterson				Martina Rodriguez	
Gloria Sloan					
Rob Peterson					
Hans Phillips					
Max Yu					

"Good start," said Sam. "You've taken the first step. I call it **populating your Referral Matrix**. The Referral Matrix is your master list of prospective referral partners. These are the people you are going to have the referral conversation with, over some period of time. The Referral Matrix is the master document of your game plan."

Jennifer responded, "Okay, Sam. I'll just go through the list and start calling them."

"Not so fast, Jen. As you've already experienced with the three folks you talked to before I left, there can be a lot of back-and-forth with the referral conversation and follow-up

The Referral Matrix is the master document of your game plan.

calls. You'll soon see this list will add up to a lot of work. The main consideration today is how you structure your game with respect to contacting the folks on your list. If this were all you had to do in your life, I'd say, 'Go for it—just go through the list and call them all.' But you have other things to do, right? Take a look at your calendar for the next couple weeks, and tell me what you've got going on."

"I'm fairly busy," said Jennifer, looking at her schedule. "I have a couple renewal meetings, two RFPs to prepare, and a couple days of internal training."

the referral code

Sam responded, "That's just what you have in your calendar. Isn't there a lot of day-to-day stuff that just pops up?"

"You've got that right, Sam. There are always client service issues, emails, calls to respond to, admin issues, and things like that. The pace is pretty frantic sometimes. Some days I come in planning to do one thing or another, and by the time I leave the office not only did I not get to my plan, I can't figure out where the time went."

"That's my point," said Sam. "Take a look at your Referral Matrix. In addition to everything else you have to do, you're going to arrange and have meetings with a number of these people, follow up with them, call the people they refer you to, and find time to meet with them as well. It's time-consuming. To do this right, you'll need to pace your game. When I talk about pacing your game I mean going after the referral activities in such a way that you participate fully, without letting any part of the process or your other work activities fall through the cracks."

"So how do I pace my game, Sam?"

"The first thing to do is prioritize your list in the order of love.

"What?"

"Order the list starting with the ones who love you the most. Take a couple minutes and do it now."

Jennifer took a few moments to think about her list and number it. As she was doing this, Sam quietly hummed The Beatle's song, "All You Need Is Love." After a moment, Jennifer began humming along with Sam, unconsciously. When she realized what was happening, she smiled at Sam, and they had a good laugh together.

"Okay, Sam. I've put my list in order of love. It's not exactly scientific, but I've done my best."

Referral Matrix in Order of Love

1. Rick Hancock (already called)
2. Nancy Hellman (already called)
3. Rita Rauche (already called)
4. Rose Samuelson
5. Rob Peterson
6. Gloria Sloan (try again)
7. Hans Phillips
8. Bill Nelson
9. Al Saunders
10. Peg Ornstein
11. Clive Lewis
12. Jack McGee
13. Bill Turner
14. Mitch Hodges
15. Pete Walsh
16. Stephen Simms
17. Leighton Wu
18. Martina Rodriguez
19. Clyde Bennett
20. Max Yu

Sam smiled, "That's fine—the Referral Code is both science and art. Tell me who on your list has given you referrals in the past."

Jennifer looked at the list. "Jack McGee over at Gateway Paper gave me a referral last year and Bill Nelson, our printer, gave me one."

"That's it? How come so few?"

Jennifer blushed and explained sheepishly, "Because I haven't asked." Then she added, "Up until now!"

the referral code

"Good point. Let's keep going. The next step is to project how many qualified referrals each person on the list will give you over the course of a year, once you do ask."

"Honestly, Sam, how could I possibly project that? I have no idea."

"Think about the people you asked since we started working together. How many did they give you?"

"Rick Hancock gave me two, but I don't see how that can help me create any kind of accurate projection. There's no guarantee. It would just be guesswork."

"What do you think a projection is? It's your best guess based on the information you have or can get, as well as certain assumptions. I'm talking about a working projection, not a pronouncement of certainty. You project, and then you make it happen with certainty."

"But I don't have any information, Sam."

"You don't? Look at the results you've gotten so far. Look at the people on your list and think about what you told me about them. Five of them are in the C-suite: CEO, CFO, CIO, COO. Don't you think they each know a number people who match your referral type? Two of the people on your list are vendors. Don't you think they do business with other companies who match your referral type? One of your personal friends on the list is the president of the Chamber of Commerce. Don't you think she knows…"

Jennifer interrupted, "Okay, Sam, I get your point."

"Remember what Stan said back at the sports bar: 'It's never about the scores until you understand the nature of the game, then it's always about the scores.' Your projections are important for two reasons: 1) they help you set up and pace your game, and 2) they give you something to measure your results by."

Jennifer asked, "What assumptions can I make in order to make these projections?"

"Number one is how much the person loves you and the work you do. Usually, those who love you the most will be more willing to go to bat for you, and more often. Second is the person's level of influence and the people they know. Remember, people like people who are like them, so it's a good bet that they know more people like them. Someone in a decision-making position probably knows other decision-makers. Third, those who have given you referrals in the past are likely to give your more in the future, especially if you ask. And remember what I said about natural promoters and connectors—the people who love to tell others about a good thing. If you have the referral conversation with a promoter or connector who loves you, you can project several referrals."

Jennifer replied, "Okay, let's start with Rick Hancock. In his last position he was COO. He really loves me and my work, and he's definitely a natural promoter. He gave me two qualified referrals and promised to refer me to his next company, so I can project three for the next 12 months."

People like people who are like them, so it's a good bet that they know more people like them.

Sam looked slightly startled "Do you think that's all you will get from him over the course of a year?"

"Actually, I haven't thought about it, Sam. Am I supposed to ask him again at some later date?"

"Absolutely. In general, you should cycle back with the people in your Referral Matrix periodically, at least every six or so months. There are certain opportune times. I call them hot spots. One of them is when you follow up with a referral source to report on what happened with the referrals he already gave you. For example, when you call Rick to tell him what happened when you met with his referral, you could ask him who else comes to mind. I'll talk to you more about hot spots another time.

"Back to Rick—how many qualified referrals do you think he might give you over the next 12 months, including the two he already gave you?"

"I already counted three. I suppose he might give me another two in the months to come. That makes five."

the referral code

"Good. And how many of those referrals do you project will result in business for you? Remember, we're talking about leads that Rick will qualify for you."

"I guess—I mean, I *project*, three deals."

"Great. Now go through your Referral Matrix and project how many referrals and deals you'll get from each person over the next 12 months."

Jennifer spent the next few minutes doing the projections. When she was done, she showed her list to Sam.

After looking the list over, Sam continued. "Now that you've made your projections, you can start to break down the work so you can set the pace of your game. It's essential that you determine how many meetings you can fit into your schedule, especially over the next 60 days while you're working this deal with Needleman. Take a look at your schedule, and think about your other work demands."

Jennifer looked at her calendar, made a few notes, and thought for a few moments.

Finally, she spoke up, "As long as I don't have to cold call, I think I can squeeze in three or four meetings a week."

"Okay. I generally recommend that you have referral conversation in-person, if possible. That way, you make sure you have someone's full attention. Sometimes, it's fine to do it on the phone. For example, if someone is in a naturally occurring state of appreciation, or if your business relationship is principally over the phone, or if you have a time or distance constraint."

For the next several minutes, Sam and Jennifer discussed how to pace her game over the next 60 days. Jennifer projected that the initial round of referral conversations would result in an average of one or two qualified referrals from each person on her list. Considering that she had time for three or four meetings per week, she decided to focus initially on 10 people on her list. Hopefully they would bring her between 10 and 20 referrals. Needleman expected each rep to have at least four prospect meetings a month, or as Sam called them 'at-bats.' Jennifer had told Roger that she would beat out the other reps, so she decided to shoot for five or six at-bats per month. That meant 10 to 12 prospect meetings over the next 60 days.

"Good plan," said Sam. "Once you start executing it, you may have to shift it a bit. You may not get meetings with everyone you call, so you may have to change your strategy and call someone else on your list. It may take some time for your people to come up with referrals and warm up those they do refer. You'll need to stay on top of your meetings and calls, be flexible, and stay patient."

Having the Referral Conversation with Friends, Family, and Associates

Once she had set her plan, Jennifer brought up the subject of how to have the referral conversation with people who had not experienced her services directly. "Sam, I have a friend, a cousin, and a business associate on my Referral Matrix. These are people who haven't personally experienced my work. It doesn't make sense to ask them, the state evoker question, 'What are some of the things that have worked for you in our working together?' How do I have a referral conversation with them?"

Sam asked, "Do you remember the purpose of the state-evoker question?"

"Sure. By having them recall what they like about working with me, they go in a state of appreciation. When people are in a state of appreciation, they're more likely to come up with referrals."

"Exactly. The same goes for people who haven't experienced your services. Instead of having them be appreciative of your work, you want them to be in a positive state about you or your relationship. It may be a state of appreciation or a heightened feeling of commonality, like when you're happy, grateful, or excited about the same thing. Sometimes, it will occur naturally."

"I think I know what you mean, Sam. Last week, I was having lunch with an old friend. I hadn't seen her in 15 years. We started talking about old times, and instantly we were laughing and relating like we hadn't missed a beat."

"Yes. You both recalled a time when there were positive feelings between you. That evoked a state of heightened rapport. By the way, the word rapport comes from the French word *rapporter*, which means 'to bring back or refer.'"

Jennifer replied, "Wow. So when I have rapport with someone, I give them an opportunity to bring referrals back to me."

"You got it!"

"Sam, is there any way to create a state of appreciation with friends if it doesn't occur naturally?"

"Yes. You can bring up old times or common experiences, like you did with your friend. Or, you can ask questions and listen with genuine interest. You can sense when there's a feeling of appreciation or connection."

"Okay, Sam. So once we've established this feeling of connection, how do I bridge the conversation to referrals?"

"You may want to gently transition the conversation to business. For example, you could ask some questions about what has been going on with your friend's business or talk a little about yours. When the time is right, you can ask for referrals. Because this is a personal relationship, you can make your referral question more informal."

"Like what?"

"You could say, 'Mary, while we're on the subject of business, I was wondering who you might know that's connected to a company I may be able to help?' You don't have to follow an exact script with personal relationships. Your friend may ask you questions about who you're looking for, or you may want to volunteer your referral type and some of the benefits of working with you. Just go with your instincts and the natural flow of the conversation."

"I get the idea. Is there anything else?"

"Yes. Though, you're not necessarily following the script I gave you for business contacts, you still need to follow a couple parts of the process: If your friend can't think of anyone in the moment, tell her, 'No problem. Why don't I go ahead follow up with you in a week or so to see who has come to mind.' If she does have a referral for you, make sure she contacts the person to pave the way for your call."

"Sounds good to me."

"So, Jen, now you have your Referral Matrix mapped out and a 60-day game plan, right?"

"Yes. I'm pretty clear on what to do. I'll get in touch if I have any questions along the way."

"Good."

Jennifer took Sam's hand, "You know, Sam, I'm really grateful for what you're doing for me. I can't tell you how helpful you've been. I feel like I've come so far in the short time we've been working together."

"You certainly have come a long way," said Sam. "It's been my pleasure."

Jennifer thought that now was a good time to practice what Sam had taught her. She decided to role-play a referral tee-up conversation with him.

"You know, Sam, next time we get together, I'd like to talk to you about who you know that could benefit from my company's IT solutions."

"Now that you mention it, I actually may know someone for you," said Sam with a gleam in his eyes. "His name is Glenn Meyers, and he owns a chain of sporting goods stores. I'll talk to him."

"That would be great, Sam. Thanks. Why don't I go ahead and take his contact information? When do you think you'll have a chance to talk with Glenn?"

"I'll call him today."

Jennifer winked and said, "Good role-playing, Sam. It's funny that you mentioned Glenn Meyers. I actually tried cold calling him several times. I never got through."

"I'm not role-playing, Jen. Glenn Meyers is a buddy of mine from way back."

the referral code

"Seriously? Wow, I thought you were just helping me practice."

"No. In fact, the referral to Glenn never occurred to me until you asked. When you expressed your gratitude, you put me into a state of appreciation too. Appreciation is contagious. See what can happen when you ask for referrals when someone is in a state of appreciation?"

"Yes, I do. I would love to connect with Glenn Meyers, Sam. It's so funny that you're going to connect me with someone I've been trying to cold call."

"It just goes to show..." Sam paused for effect.

"What?" Jen asked.

"Warm beats cold every time."

all hell

Jennifer started working her Referral Matrix the next day. Within 24 hours, she scheduled lunches with six people on her list: three clients, a vendor, a business associate, and a friend.

Sam called her to say he talked to his friend Glenn Meyers and he was expecting her call. When Jennifer called Glenn, he invited her to the corporate office to talk about her services.

Jennifer looked at her schedule. Seven meetings scheduled for the next two weeks. *Good start,* she told herself.

Then all hell broke loose.

One of her biggest clients, Swenson's Supermarkets, called with a major service issue related to a merger with another company. Within the next three weeks, they wanted Jennifer to create an RFP for merging the two systems. It was a complicated project filled with uncertainties and issues that required research and discussion. This project would put a significant demand on her time and energy. Jennifer wondered how she could fit in the lunches, follow-ups, meetings, and still do all the work necessary for the RFP.

That evening, she went home and found water all over the bathroom floor and seeping into the bedroom. After mopping up, she called a plumber, who instructed her to turn off the main line. Neil was out of town at a conference, so Jennifer had to deal with the plumbing problem herself.

The following day, Jennifer waited for the plumber until noon—two hours after his scheduled time. When he finally arrived and explored the situation, he told Jennifer that the main line was broken and the pipes needed to be replaced. His estimate was close to $10,000. Until the main line was fixed, Jennifer and Neil would have no water.

Jennifer wanted a second opinion and another estimate, which would kill yet another day. She decided to work at home the next day so she could have another plumber take a look. Fortunately, the second plumber gave a much lower estimate. Unfortunately, she was falling behind in her work and becoming increasingly stressed.

When Jennifer arrived at work the following day, she found out that 15 percent of the company's employees had just been laid off, including two of her closest friends. As she said good-bye to them, she fought to hold back the tears. Her stress level shot through the roof.

Just before lunch, Needleman called her into his office and asked her how she was doing with her plan. Jennifer informed him of her progress. Though she was overwhelmed by all that was happening, she assured him that she had everything under control.

Needleman said, "I hope you'll have good news for me over the next several weeks. Between you, me, and the fence post, today may be only the beginning of our right-sizing."

Jennifer thought, *I hate that euphemism. Why doesn't he call it what it really is: layoffs.*

After leaving Needleman's office, she headed to the first client lunch resulting from her referral calls. While driving, she used Instant Recall[5] to put herself into a state of calm confidence. Her meeting was with Rob Peterson, the COO of a commercial real estate company.

She spent some time asking about new developments in Rob's business and how the company's IT services were working out. When she had the referral conversation with him, Rob said he would gladly recommend her, but he had to think about who he knew that would meet her referral criteria. She told him she would follow up in a week or so.

---

5 Described in *Sell the Feeling.*

She went straight from lunch to meet with Glenn Meyers, Sam's friend. She had already prepared for the meeting by researching his company—Step 1 of *Sell the Feeling*. Her closing point was to set up a technical analysis.

At the meeting, she followed the remaining five steps of *Sell the Feeling*, and Glenn revealed numerous complaints with his current IT service. He readily agreed to the tech analysis. Jennifer left the meeting feeling great.

The next day, she arrived at the office at 5 AM to work on the Swenson Supermarket RFP. She closed the door and worked steadily until her next lunch meeting with another of her best clients.

She left lunch with two referrals and promised to follow up with her client next week, once he had a chance to make contact and warm up the leads.

When Jennifer returned to the office, there was a voice-mail from a member of her service team asking her to call him ASAP. Jennifer sensed tension in his voice and called him immediately on his cell phone. He was on-site at a client's office performing routine server maintenance. The company's IT manager was ranting about recent system problems and accused the technician and Jennifer's company of being incompetent.

This is all I need on a Friday afternoon, thought Jennifer.

She called the client and decided it would be best if she visited the site personally, even though it meant facing rush-hour traffic. Upon arriving, she learned that the issue was due to operator error and unrelated to IT services. The technician had tried to convey this to the IT manager, but somehow the conversation had gone astray. Jennifer explained the issue and smoothed all the ruffled feathers.

When she got into her car, she turned on the radio and heard a reporter talking about the latest bad economic news. *I'm on a mission,* she thought. *There's no way I'm going participate in the societal trance now.* She immediately switched to a music station.

As she reflected back on her week she thought, *What a rollercoaster ride!* She had tackled the Swenson RFP, spent two days dealing with a plumbing emergency, seen her good friends lose their jobs, and appeased a client who had gone off the deep end. On the other hand, she had faithfully worked her Referral Matrix, received a few potential referrals, and had a successful meeting with Glenn Meyers. She was exhausted and felt like she needed to unwind.

Great timing! Her next stop was Mario's Restaurant for a dinner date with her friend Rose. She rolled up her windows, cranked up the music, and did her best to forget about the hassles of her week and rise above the bumper-to-bumper traffic.

Chapter 21

the friends/family
conversation

jennifer and Rose met as college roommates and had continued their friendship ever since. Though they only saw each other once or twice a year, they considered themselves close friends.

In a booth at Mario's Restaurant, they ordered drinks before dinner and talked about their families, mutual friends, and old times. During their conversation, Jennifer felt a mutual feeling of connection and appreciation.

"Even though we don't see each other that often, Jen, it always feels like we take up right where we left off," said Rose. They smiled at each other and instinctively reached for each other's hand.

Despite this gesture and the good feelings, Jennifer was a little uneasy about having the referral conversation with Rose.

Am I about to cross a boundary here? What if she thinks this a breach of our friendship? She might think I set up this dinner just to pump her for business leads.

Then Jennifer remembered something Sam had said awhile back about the nature of the game: by and large, people refer you to pay it forward.

She decided to transition to the topic of business by asking Rose about her public relations firm and her position as president of her local chamber of commerce.

the referral code

As Rose dished out the latest news, Jennifer listened with genuine interest. They went back and forth for a while on the subject of Rose's firm and some of her juicier clients.

After a few minutes, Rose said to Jennifer, "Tell me what's going on in your business. How are you guys faring in this economy?"

Jennifer briefed Rose on the latest happenings. She said that despite the downturn in business, things were picking up on her end. Still sensing the mutual feeling of connection between them, Jennifer decided it was time to ask.

She was about to say, 'Rose I'd like to ask you a favor,' but she remembered the referral conversation was not about a favor—instead, it was an opportunity for Rose to help people she cared about by introducing them to Jennifer.

Since Rose was a friend, Jennifer used an informal version of the referral question: "Rose, as long as we're talking about business, I was wondering who you might know that could use our help."

"Let me think for a moment," said Rose. "Tell me more about who you're looking for."

Jennifer told Rose about her referral type and gave her examples of the kinds of companies she worked with and the benefits they had gained.

Rose responded, "I can see that you may be able to help some of the companies that I have good relationships with. I'll look through my database. Call me on Monday, okay?"

"That would be great, Rose. Thanks."

Rose replied, "And while we're on the subject, if you ever run across someone who could use some great PR, please think of me."

Jennifer smiled to herself. In light of all she had learned from Sam, Jennifer couldn't help but notice how weak Rose's request felt. Instead of asking **whom** she knew, Rose had couched her request in vague terms by using the if-then approach.

Well, at least she's asking, thought Jen.

"I'd be happy to refer you, Rose. Tell me who you're looking for." Jennifer asked a number of questions to drill down to Rose's referral type, the benefits her clients got from working with her firm, and the kinds of situations that would trigger the need for her services.

"Jennifer, I really appreciate your questions. You're actually helping me to better identify my niche."

Rose was a good friend and a consummate professional. Jennifer vowed to do her best to refer her. She couldn't think of anyone that needed Rose's services now, but she decided to look through her database over the weekend.

On Sunday, Jennifer scoured through her database, looking for people that fit Rose's referral type. She found a couple of possibilities and decided to call them on Monday before following up with Rose. It turned out that one was already working with a PR firm and the other was not interested.

She called Rose that afternoon, as promised.

"Jen, thanks for calling. I had such a good time with you the other night. I have four names for you. Are you ready?"

"Great, Rose." Jennifer took down the names, and asked some questions to better understand and qualify the leads.

Rose said, "Go ahead and call them. Tell them I referred you. If you have any trouble getting through, just let me know."

"Thanks, Rose. I really appreciate these referrals. In my experience, it's best if **you** warm them up for me. Could you give them a call to pave the way for me to contact them?"

"Sure," said Rose. "I can see why that would be better. I'll have time to call them tomorrow. Give me a call on Wednesday or Thursday."

"Will do. By the way, I looked through my database to see who might be a good fit for you. I called a couple of people I know and they were dead-ends, at

the referral code

least for the time being. One of the people I called is already working with a PR agency. I told him about you and asked him to give me a call if he has any hiccups with his current PR firm. I'll keep trying."

"Not a problem, Jen. Thanks for trying. I appreciate it. Just keep me in mind. I know where to find you."

Jennifer was truly excited. *Four potential referrals*, she thought. *This stuff really works! I just wish I could come up with someone for Rose.*

Then it hit her: Sam.

She dialed his number. "Sam, I just had the referral conversation with my friend Rose, and she came up with four leads for me! She's going to warm them up for me in the next couple of days. This is so cool!"

"Way to go, Jen!"

"Listen, I was thinking—Rose is a brilliant publicist. Have you ever thought about publicizing the work you do? I'm sure she could help you create some buzz that would lead to more seminar business."

"Sounds interesting. I've been considering hiring a marketing specialist, but I haven't thought about the publicity route. Why don't you give me Rose's number, and I'll give her a call."

After giving Sam Rose's contact information, Jennifer said, "I will call Rose and let her know to expect your call."

Later, she called Rose and told her all about Sam.

"Thanks, Jen. He sounds like he has an interesting story with several potential media angles. I bet I can help him. I look forward to his call."

When Jennifer got off the phone, she felt a warm glow. She smiled and took a couple minutes to bask in the feeling.

So this is what it feels like to pay it forward.

Chapter 22

the referral conversation— start to finish

Over the next two weeks, Jennifer juggled the Swenson RFP, client service issues, and meetings and follow-up calls with people on her Referral Matrix.

She called her friend Rose, who gave her the go-ahead to call two of her four referrals. The other two were not good candidates at this time. Once Rose explained why, Jennifer agreed that they weren't qualified leads.

I'm glad Rose made those calls. She saved me a lot of time and energy.

Jennifer called Rose's two qualified leads and set up meetings.

In addition to the meetings, the follow-ups, the RFP, and everything else, Jennifer had to deal with numerous emails, phone calls, and a whole host of interruptions. And underneath it all was the pressure of her challenge with Needleman.

By the end of the first 30 days, she had met with seven people from her Referral Matrix. She had planned to meet with 10, but two were unavailable until the next month and one had to reschedule at the last minute.

All told, she had received five referrals, but had only met with three. She was still waiting on her referral partners to warm up the other two. In addition, three of the clients she met with were still thinking about whom they could refer. Jennifer planned to follow up with them the next week to see who had come to mind.

Needleman had reserved the right to cancel their agreement if Jennifer fell below four at-bat meetings at the end of the first month. Jennifer had only had three at-bats so far, but she expected to meet with two more referrals as soon as her clients warmed them up.

She met with Needleman in his office and explained her results. She told him that she fully expected to finish the next month with at least six additional prospect meetings. Roger seemed distracted and somewhat indifferent.

"Just go ahead and keep to your plan," was all he had to say.

Strange, Jennifer thought. *He usually has plenty of opinions to offer. I wonder what's up.*

Regardless of Roger's seeming indifference, Jennifer knew she had to maximize her referral activities over the next 30 days. She had seen the monthly sales report, and two of her fellow account reps were already ahead of her, with four prospect meetings each. She was determined to win this game, and to do so, she figured she would need to rack up six or seven additional prospect meetings. That number of meetings in a month was almost unheard of in her company, especially during tough economic times.

Jennifer was highly competitive and couldn't stand the thought of losing. Given the amount of other work she had to do, she could hardly imagine pulling off five or six at-bats in 30 days. She started worrying and began to feel overwhelmed with all she had to do. Her shoulders and neck were all knotted up, and she wasn't sleeping well. She had not been to the gym in a month and she desperately needed to burn off some stress.

Damn, I really need a break. Jennifer packed her things, left work in the middle of the day, and headed to the gym.

As she ran on the treadmill, she continued to stress over all she had to do. Then she remembered what Neil said, 'Shut up, focus up, and do the work!'

That's still great advice. She decided to change her state. She remembered a time she felt free and easy-going. It was on a dinner date with Neil, early in their relationship. As she vividly recalled that evening, she instantly felt better.

She decided to put work on ice, physically and mentally, for the rest of the day. Tomorrow she would shut up, focus up, and do the work. She called Neil and arranged a dinner date that evening. When she finished her workout, she was able to squeeze in an hour-long massage at a local spa. The tension in her neck and shoulders melted away.

Jennifer and Neil had a romantic dinner at their favorite restaurant. She got a good night's sleep and awoke the next day refreshed and ready to focus up and do the work.

That day, she went to meet with one of the clients on her Referral Matrix: Hans Phillips, the founder and CEO of Phillips Energy Partners, a company that specialized in bio-fuel research and development. Hans was a brilliant scientist and a savvy entrepreneur. He had a reputation for being aloof, and at times, arrogant.

Sometimes Jennifer felt intimidated by Hans, but she put him on her list nevertheless. Her team had worked closely with Hans to develop an innovative IT infrastructure that he designed. Jennifer knew that Hans appreciated her and the work her team did. She also knew that his company had numerous strategic partnerships with companies that matched her referral type.

She set up a meeting to discuss the next phase of Hans' IT master plan. She brought two members of her service team with her. The meeting went well. Though he was matter-of-fact as usual, Jennifer could tell that Hans was pleased with her and her team. When the meeting was over, she asked to speak to Hans alone.

"Hans, we've come a long way since we first discussed your IT vision over a year ago. I was wondering, what are some of the things that have worked for you in our working together?"

Hans responded matter-of-factly, "Well, you executed my plan, didn't you?"

"Yes, we did." Jennifer knew in advance that she might have to coax the appreciation out of Hans. "What was it about how we executed your plan that worked so well for you?" She knew that this question would begin to intensify the state of appreciation.

Hans paused and considered the question before answering, "Your team has been dependable and you are responsive whenever I need something. You took my lead and carried the ball across the goal line."

the referral code

Hans was not the kind of person to openly display emotion, so Jennifer decided to try once more. "What else has worked for you in our working together?"

"Jennifer, I know I can be a tough customer at times. My standards are high and I expect everyone I work with to be at the top of their profession. Some vendors have a hard time working with us because I'm so demanding. Despite a few hiccups we had in the build-out phase, I think you are a highly professional organization with the resources we need."

As Hans spoke, Jennifer took notes. Before asking the referral question, she took a quick look at what she had written. She decided to tailor her question using some of Hans' key words.

"Hans, I was wondering, who do you know that is connected to a company with two hundred or more employees that can benefit from the same kind of dependable, responsive, professional service you just described?"

Hans looked Jennifer straight in the eye and said, "I see. You are looking for referrals, aren't you?"

Jennifer felt a little anxious. Did Hans think she was buttering him up? Had she been found out? Hans was always direct in his communication.

Jennifer decided to be direct in her response: "Yes, Hans. I'm looking for companies that you can help by referring us."

"I have no problem referring you."

"That's good to hear. Who do you know, Hans?"

"I tell you what Jennifer—you've done a good job, and I want to think about this."

Jennifer replied, "No problem. Why don't I give you a call in a week or so to see who has come to mind."

"Yes, that will do. Tell me a little more about the kinds of industries you service."

Jennifer spent the next couple of minutes describing some of her client profiles and how the companies benefited from her services. When she left, she felt happy with herself and somewhat relieved. Hans was a tough nut to crack, and she had handled it well.

At the same time, she was anxious, realizing that she had just over three weeks left in her agreement with Needleman. By the time she cycled back with Hans, she would have only two weeks to contact and meet with any referrals he might give her. She wished she had an extra few weeks.

The next Wednesday, she called Hans. His assistant said that he had just left town to attend a conference and would be gone the rest of the week. Jennifer felt a knot in the pit of her stomach. This was going to take longer than she had hoped. She tapped the Phillie doll's bouncing head to remind herself of Sam's three Ps: pacing, patience, and persistence.

That night, Jennifer received an email:

```
Heard you called. At conference. Scouting for you. Back
Monday. Please call then. —Hans
```

When she called Monday, Hans wasn't in, so she left him a voicemail. At 1:30 AM, he sent her a four-word email:

```
Very busy. Haven't forgotten. —Hans
```

When she read the email that morning and saw what time he sent it, she thought, *He really must be busy. I don't want to bug him. There's not much I can do at this point, other than wait to hear back.*

Wait a minute! She realized she was about to give up control of the game. Instead, she sent Hans an email:

```
No problem, Hans. Why don't I follow up with you next week
if I haven't heard back from you by then. That will work,
won't it?
Best,
Jennifer
```

the referral code

If she didn't hear back from Hans in a week, she would pick up the phone and call him.

Meanwhile, Jennifer met another person on her Referral Matrix: Jack, her printer. He gave her two names and agreed to warm up the referrals. Jennifer said she would call back in a week or so to follow up.

The next Monday, she called Jack. He had not yet warmed up the leads, but he said he would get to it by the end of the week. Jennifer was juggling her routine work, the Swenson RFP, and referral follow-ups. She realized that she was starting to lose track of where she was with the various referral sources and leads. She created a spreadsheet to keep track.[6]

Sam wasn't kidding when he said how much time this would take and that I need to pace my game, she thought.

The following Tuesday, she called Hans. This time he picked up. She got right to the point.

"Hi Hans, I'm calling to follow up on our conversation to see who has come to mind."

"Sorry for not getting back to you, Jennifer. I had some major fires to put out last week. I've given it some thought, and I have someone who may fit your profile. His name is Ravi Singh. He runs the data center for Yang Enterprises, a worldwide electronics distribution network. They're a big outfit. If you land it, it could be a huge account for you."

After taking Ravi's contact information Jennifer said, "Thanks, Hans. Why don't you go ahead and give Ravi a call and tell him some of the things that have worked for you in our working together."

"I don't think that will be necessary. Just give him a call and tell him I recommended you."

Hans sounded rushed. Jennifer didn't want to push him too hard, but she knew it would be better if he paved the way for her.

---

6 The referral tracking spreadsheet is part of the complimentary bonus that comes with this book. For more information, go www.ReferralCodeBonus.info.

She decided to go after it one more time, "Hans, I usually have better results if I have a warm introduction. If you don't have time to call him, could you go ahead and send him an email introducing me and telling him a couple of things that have worked for you in our working together, and let him know I'll be calling? You can copy me on the email, and I'll take it from there."

"That I can do."

"Hans, I know how busy you are. When do you think you'll have time?"

"I'll do it tonight."

"Perfect. Thanks, Hans." Normally, Jennifer would have asked him, "Who else comes to mind?" but she sensed that he was anxious to get off the phone, so she hesitated. Then she remembered what Sam had said to do when the timing wasn't right: tee-up the referral conversation.

"Hans, in the next couple of weeks, I'd like to talk to you about who else you know that could benefit from the same kind of service we've given you."

Hans chuckled, "No problem, Jennifer. By the way, I like your persistence."

Sure enough, at 11:30 that night, Jennifer received a copy of Hans' email to Ravi:

Ravi,

I've got someone I think you should meet. Her name is Jennifer Stewart, and she's a senior account exec at Pacific IT Solutions. They built out our IT infrastructure and helped design business solutions for that framework. They also provide us ongoing support and maintenance. Jennifer and her team do a superb job and I highly recommend them. I took the liberty of giving her your number. You can expect her call. —Hans

She emailed Hans back to say thanks and tell him she would let him know how things panned out with Ravi.

the referral code

Jennifer called Ravi the next day. Once she established the potential need for her services, she set up a meeting with him two weeks later. She then emailed Hans to tell him what had happened and that she would let him know the results of the meeting.

Her meeting with Ravi would occur after the 60-day challenge, but that was okay—based on her research and what Hans told her, she knew this referral could represent a major opportunity for her and the company. She would take this one any way she could get it.

Jennifer took stock of where she was. With a little less than two weeks to go in her agreement with Needleman, she had received a total of nine qualified referrals and had met with seven of them. She had two meetings set for the next week. If everything went as planned, she would end up with nine at-bat meetings for the 60-day period—more than three times as many meetings as she had set up in two and a half months of calling hundreds of cold leads.

Would she win her 60-day challenge? She had been so consumed in her own work that she hadn't had time to check in on how the others in her department were doing. With 10 days still to go, there was no telling what might happen.

out with the old

f ortunately, the next week went extremely well. Jennifer met with two prospects, one of whom said he would seriously consider moving forward with a technical analysis. That week, Jennifer's service team performed a technical analysis for Glenn Meyers Sport Stores, the company Sam had referred.

The 60-day challenge was officially complete. All told, Jennifer met with nine prospects, five of whom had asked her to respond to RFPs. One prospect was in the process of gathering information that Jennifer had requested, and three were interested in following up with her at a later date. Jennifer was hopeful—as Sam said, delays are not denials.

First thing Thursday morning, Jennifer emailed Needleman the results of her 60-day challenge. She didn't hear anything back, so later that afternoon, she wandered by his office. Roger's executive assistant told her that he had left town and wouldn't be back until the following week.

Strange, thought Jennifer. *He didn't tell anyone he was leaving.*

The next morning, Jennifer received an email from Needleman:

Jennifer,
I got the email with your results. You did a great job pulling in 9 meetings. However, Frank Flexner had 10. I'm at my ranch in Texas for a little R&R and will be back in the office on Tuesday. We can discuss then.

Best,
Roger

the referral code

Jennifer's heart sank. *I put everything I had into this. How did Frank beat me out? Does this mean I have to go back to cold calling? Why is Roger gone with no notice, and why is he keeping me hanging on like this?*

Frank Flexner had been with the company over 10 years. He was the top producer and a cold-calling maniac. The rest of the department called him 'Frankie Fingers' because he loved dialing for dollars and had built a successful career around it.

Jennifer decided to have a little talk with Frank. She was curious about his results and how he pulled off 10 meetings. She wandered down to his office and poked her head into his doorway.

"Yo, Jennifer. What's up, sugar?" Frankie Fingers was up, as always.

"How ya' been, Frank?"

"Absolutely incredible. You?"

"I'm good. Frank, I heard from Roger that you finished pretty strong these past two months."

"I did." Frank held up his right hand, wiggled his fingers, and winked.

Jennifer smiled disingenuously, thinking, *Is this a cue for me bow down to his mighty dialing digits?* Jennifer liked and respected Frank, but sometimes he could be a little smug .

"Frank, I have a question, if you don't mind."

"Not at all, Jenzzie. Ask away."

"How many new prospect meetings did you book this month and last?"

Frank opened his notebook and looked at a couple of pages, before answering, "10."

"I'm curious, Frank—how did you get all those meetings?" Jennifer tilted her head, cocked her eyebrows, and pointed to her raised hand as she wiggled her fingers.

"Frank laughed, then said, "Eight were from cold calling, and two came from referrals, thanks in part to you!"

"What do you mean, Frank?"

"I was in the executive committee meeting about a month ago. Needleman was telling the CEO about how you've been rippin' it up with referrals. I get referrals sometimes, but I never tried asking directly like you've been doing. I decided to try it myself. I called up a bunch of my current and past clients and asked them who they knew. I call it warm calling."

Frank went on to tell Jennifer that he was finding it increasingly difficult to get through to decision-makers via cold calling.

"I like this referral thing," he said. "When you have time, I'd like to take you to lunch and find out more about your techniques."

After a bit more chitchat, she headed back to her office.

Jennifer was steaming. *That son-of-a-bitch, Needleman. He said this would be our secret. He leaked it to Frank, and Frank took my game and used it to beat me!*

Jennifer stewed for an hour our two. When she got home, she told Neil what had happened.

"Okay, so he beat you," Neil said. "Get over it. Forget about this little contest for the moment and think about the bigger picture. I think you've more than proved your point. Now Needleman has even more evidence that the Referral Code system works. You're the second top-performing rep for the 60-day period. That's awesome! And don't forget that Frank has been the top dog for years. And now he's using your strategy. What do you think Needleman is going to do? Send you back to the cold-calling salt mines?"

"You're right, Neil. I'm also going to tell Needleman that if Frank hadn't used my referral play, I would have beaten him. Anyway, I'm tired of stressing about this. I did a good job and like you said, I proved my point."

the referral code

"You did a **great** job, and you **more** than proved your point, especially considering that you just started employing the referral strategy about three months ago."

"Thanks, Neil. You're right. Let's open a bottle of champagne. I'm ready to celebrate and enjoy our weekend!"

The following Tuesday, Needleman was back in the office. Jennifer emailed his assistant and set a time to meet with him that afternoon.

Roger ushered Jennifer into his office and closed the door.

"Jennifer, I want you to know that even though Frank Flexner set the most meetings, your point about building business by referrals was well-taken."

"Apparently so. Frank told me he heard about what I was doing from you, and he appropriated my strategy. It's not like I have a patent on this, but come on, Roger—we had an agreement that this 60-day challenge was to be our little secret. If Frank hadn't gone after referrals, I would have won."

"Yes, I did let the cat out of the bag, but let me explain. As you know, Jennifer, our sales have not been what we hoped, even with the increased cold calling. Our third-quarter results were almost 25 percent below expectations.

Roger continued, "A major topic of last month's executive committee meeting was what we could do to improve sales. At one point, the CEO Kenny Dillenberg asked what other sales approaches we could consider in addition to cold calling. Knowing the progress you were already making, I decided to tell Kenny about what you were doing. After all, if I had any ideas that could help the company, it was my responsibility to bring them up. Both Kenny and Frank asked a number of questions about your approach. Obviously, Frank listened well."

"Why didn't you tell me, Roger?"

Roger shuffled a bit in his chair. He reached for a box of mints on his desk and offered Jennifer one. She declined.

"I apologize, Jennifer. To tell you the truth, I meant to tell you, but I've been a bit distracted. My plan to invigorate sales hasn't worked out as expected. No one knows this yet, but I've tendered my resignation."

Jennifer was surprised, "You're kidding!" She was beginning to understand Roger's recent disconnect.

"Truth is, I am being allowed to bow out, gracefully. The board wants to re-organize the sales department. Dillenberg is temporarily going to take the department under his wing while they search for a new executive VP of sales."

"Roger, I'm so sorry," said Jennifer. She was shocked that she actually meant it.

"Thanks, Jennifer. I haven't told anyone else. Please keep this quiet. It won't become public until the end of the week."

"I'll keep it to myself. You must feel terrible, Roger."

"I'd be lying if I said I'm not disappointed. On the other hand, I've been around the block enough times to see that the company needs to explore another direction. It's clear that something needs to change in how the company approaches sales in the current economy and maybe even beyond that. The old ways just aren't working anymore."

Roger continued, "I think you're onto something with this referral strategy. After all, the numbers don't lie. I shared your results with Kenny at our meeting this morning. He was quite impressed that you booked nine meetings, and that you sold three technical analyses. I also told him about your upcoming meeting with Yang Enterprises. He wants to talk with you."

"Thanks, Roger. I'd welcome the opportunity to speak with him. By the way, do you think I can continue with my program?"

"At this point, it's up to Kenny, but I can't imagine he would want to tamper with what is obviously working so well."

Jennifer was excited and relieved.

"By the way, Jennifer, how many calls did you make to leads to get those nine meetings?"

"About 25 calls," Jennifer told Roger.

"Amazing! Frank made something like five hundred calls in the past two months to get his 10 meetings." Roger tapped some numbers into his calculator, then looked up, wide-eyed. "This is mind-boggling. You had a 64 percent pull-through. I've come to expect only one to three percent!"

Jennifer replied, "I guess you could say that warm beats cold. By the way Roger, I have another three or four referral leads that I haven't had an opportunity to connect with yet."

"You must have some strong relationships, Jennifer. I salute you."

Jennifer wanted to leap for joy, but under the circumstances felt it would be insensitive.

"Roger, I don't know what to say. Actually I do—thanks for letting me do my little experiment."

Roger gave a hint of a smile. "You are most welcome. I'm glad you did so well. I wish you continued success. You'll be hearing from Dillenberg soon."

Jennifer paused and considered what to say next. "Roger, you've been so helpful to me. I'm sorry you're leaving under these circumstances."

"That's okay, Jennifer. I'm a tough old dog, and I'll be fine. Now if you'll excuse me, I have number of things to do to prepare for my exit. Would you mind closing the door on your way out?"

As Jennifer got up to leave, she spotted a trace of moisture in Roger's eyes. She also noticed that the 16-point buck head that used to be mounted on the wall behind Roger's desk now rested in a packing crate next to the door.

Jennifer knew that Roger had tried his best to rekindle the sales department, but his cold-calling initiative seemed inefficient and outdated. More and more, people were counting on their relationships to recommend products, services, and vendors.

Though Jennifer personally hated cold calling, she acknowledged that it did work for some people, in certain situations, or in some industries. After all, Frank loved cold calling and had used it to build a successful business. But even Frank said it was getting more and more difficult to get through to decision-makers via cold calling. Most of the reps Jennifer had spoken with disliked dialing for dollars. And she knew from personal experience that most people on the receiving end of cold calls disliked them as much, if not more than, the people making them.

Though Jennifer had disagreed with Roger over his strategy and management style, he had listened to her and taken a chance by allowing her to run with her referral strategy. In fact, had Roger not mandated the cold-calling program, Jennifer would not have taken on the Referral Code. Back in her office, she teared up a bit herself. She knew that beneath that gritty, tough-talking facade, Roger was hurting.

hot spots and social media

though she felt bad for Roger, Jennifer was upbeat about her recent accomplishments and her future. Yes, Frank had gotten more meetings, but Jennifer knew she had proved herself and the effectiveness of the Referral Code system. Based on her performance and Roger's comments, she was hopeful that the CEO would let her continue growing her business in a way that was obviously working.

Things were good at home as well. Neil had recovered nicely and was back at work. He had absorbed much of Sam's system through Jennifer and had employed the referral conversation with a couple of his own clients. It worked—Neil had received three referrals so far, two of which turned into business.

When Jennifer met Sam at Patty's Diner on Friday morning, she told him about her conversation with Needleman and Hans' referral to Ravi Singh.

"Great work, Jen," said Sam, beaming. "You've come a long way. I knew you had it in you."

"Thanks, Sam. You're a great coach!"

"Thanks—I appreciate that. Too bad about Needleman, but the old ways are dying out. People have become much more savvy and discriminating. They're looking for ways to cut through the clutter of vendors that are constantly approaching them from all sides. Relationships are more important now than ever. Receiving a good referral from someone you know and trust is so much better than a cold call. Like I always say, warm beats cold every time."

Jennifer asked, "So where do we go from here, Sam?"

the referral code

"You've learned almost everything I have to teach you about the Referral Code. There's just one more thing we need to cover: going back to the well."

"What do you mean, Sam?"

"Once you've asked someone for referrals, you'll want to go back periodically and ask again. Even if you asked someone and didn't receive a referral, circumstances may be different later. Things are always changing—your referral partners may develop new relationships or they may become aware of new needs with their existing relationships. Besides, it would take a heck of a long time to exhaust the possibilities in your relationships' connections. Rule Number One is that you have to ask. Rule Number Two is to keep asking. Unless you ask again and again, I promise you that you will miss out on opportunities."

Rule Number One is that you have to ask. Rule Number Two is to keep asking. Unless you ask again and again, you will miss out on opportunities.

➡

"I'm glad you brought this up, Sam. I had a situation the other day with my client Hans when he referred me to Ravi. I was ready to ask him for that second cookie, but I sensed the timing wasn't right. He seemed rushed, so I decided not to ask in that moment. I used the tee-up instead. I figure I can talk with him again once I meet with Ravi."

"Good thinking, Jen. It was good that you listened to your instincts about Hans. Asking for referrals is both a science and an art. Now that you know the system, be sure to pay attention to your instincts. There are a lot of nuances in human behavior and dynamics. Your instincts will give you clues about when and how to act."

Jennifer asked, "So in general, when and how do I go back to the well?"

"Personally, I think you can go back to the people who love you every three to six months. There are certain situations or events that provide a natural opportunity to ask again. I call these **hot spots**."

Jennifer asked, "For instance?"

166

"We've talked about some of them already. Right after someone gives you a referral, you can thank him then ask who else comes to mind. You have a hot spot anytime the referral moves forward—for example, after you talk or meet with prospect, agree to do an RFP, or convert a prospect into a client. Let your client know what happened, then ask for more referrals.

"When someone gives you a referral to someone he knows and cares about, he has a vested interest in the outcome. If the outcome is positive, your referrer gets to feel good about it too. Remember: people refer you to pay it forward to those they care about, and when things go well they get to be the hero. When you let a referrer know that you are taking good care of someone he or she referred to you, it will evoke a state of appreciation. That state provides you the opportunity to go back to the well."

Jennifer asked, "What if someone gives me a referral and it doesn't turn into business?"

"That can be a hot spot, as well. You can call the referrer to tell her you spoke with the referral. Tell her that it was a good referral and you really appreciate it even though it didn't pan out to business this time. Then ask again."

"Are there any other hot spots, Sam?"

"Yes. The rule of thumb is you can ask whenever your referral partner is in a naturally occurring state of appreciation about you, your company, or your relationship. That could occur any time —for instance, at a meeting, on the phone, or if and when you see each other socially. Look for any cues that tell you that the person is in a state of appreciation."

At that moment, the waitress arrived at their table and served them breakfast.

A moment later, Patty walked up, "Hi Jennifer. Hi Sam. Everything okay?"

Sam answered, "Just fine, Patty. Good to see you!"

Patty turned to Jennifer, "Thanks so much for sending in your friend Rose and your client Rick. Rose has been here two or three times. We love you for it!"

the referral code

Patty turned to the waitress, "Irene, please bring these good folks a couple slices of our fresh butter pecan coffee cake, on the house."

Sam smiled and whispered to Jen, "Not only do you get to be the hero, you get dessert on top of it!"

After Patty and Irene left, Jennifer asked, "Sam, when I go back to the well, should I intentionally evoke a state of appreciation? Can I just use the state-evoker question again with the same person?"

"Obviously, it's always best to ask when the person is in a state of appreciation, but I wouldn't use the state-evoker more than once with the same person. Once you've asked the state-evoker question, asking it again may seem contrived. However, you can bring up other things to evoke a state of appreciation. For example, you could refer to some service or benefit you provided your client or some positive result you created and have a discussion around that. Or, if it applies, you could bring up some enjoyable time you spent together in a context outside of business."

"Give me an example, Sam."

"Okay, I'll be you." Sam took on a higher-pitched voice as if he were playing Jennifer. "So Joe, we calculated that the new system we installed has cut your average transaction cost by 20 percent. What do you think about that?"

Sam lowered his voice to play the part of Joe, "I think it's terrific, Jennifer. I'm so glad to hear it. This project has exceeded our expectations."

Sam, as Jennifer, replied, "Thanks, Joe. I knew you'd be happy. Hey, I was wondering," Sam paused for a moment as if contemplating, "Who do you know that could benefit from the same level of IT services and cost savings that you've experienced?"

Jennifer responded, "That's good, Sam. I do have one concern about all this: Do you think I might be perceived as pushy if I keep asking for more referrals once someone has given me one?"

"If you ask in a pushy way, yes. But you're sensitive and polite, so I doubt you will ever have that problem. Just use your instincts and be sure to use hot spots and naturally occurring states of appreciation as opportunities to ask."

"Good. I'll go back to the well with Hans once I've met with Ravi."

"I'm sure you will."

Gifts and Acknowledgements

"I have another question, Sam. Should I do anything special to thank my referral partners, like sending handwritten notes, gifts, and things like that?"

Sam answered, "I think personalized, handwritten notes are a nice touch. Alternatively, you can call or do something special for them. Gifts can be good, especially when someone gives you a great referral that pans out. For example, you may want to send Hans a gift in appreciation for the referral to Ravi once you get the business. Just be sure the gift is appropriate for the person. For example, you should be careful with alcohol—you don't want to send a bottle of wine to someone who doesn't drink.

"Also, it's great to send a gift that matches someone's interests. You know I love baseball and that I've been a Yankees fan all my life, right? A client once sent me an original photo of Mickey Mantle, Yogi Berra, and Roger Maris. Talk about a feeling of appreciation! If you need advice as to what to send, check with someone that knows the referrer, like an assistant or secretary.

"Over time, you will find that certain people become what I call **key referral sources**. These are the people that continually give you referrals—they might be considered your biggest fans. You want to treat these folks with kid-glove care. You can periodically send them gifts, take them out, treat them to an afternoon of golf, or send them and a guest to a fine restaurant, sports event, play, or concert. With your key referral sources, you don't have to wait until they give you a referral. Surprise them by sending a token of your appreciation when they least expect it. They'll love you for it, and it will deepen the feelings of appreciation and increase loyalty."

Sam looked off to the side and muttered to himself, "But come to think of it, gifts aren't everyone's loyalty trigger."

Jennifer asked, "What are loyalty triggers?"

"Loyalty triggers are the specific things that trigger a longer-lasting loyalty from your existing clients and referral sources. Think about it Jen—what if you knew how to secure a client's loyalty over longer periods of time?"

"That would be great. Can you show me how, Sam?"

"That's a whole other training. It will have to wait until another day. It's the subject of my next book, right after the one about the Referral Code."

"I can't wait, Sam."

"One more thing. If you're going to send a gift, be sure to make it a classy one. If you're sending a bottle of wine, make it a really good one. If you're taking or sending your client out to dinner, be sure to choose a fine restaurant."

"Great advice, Sam. Rick Hancock has become a key referral source for me. I'll do something for him in the near future."

Using Social Media

"Sam, I have another question for you: A lot of people are using social media tools on the Web as part of their business development. Do you know anything about this?" Sam was in his late 60s, so Jennifer figured he was relatively 'old-school' and would know little, if anything, about social media.

Sam responded with a twinkle in his eye, "Do you mean things like Facebook, LinkedIn, Plaxo, and Twitter?"

Jennifer smiled and replied, "You surprise me, Sam!"

"Why? Do you have a limiting belief that says an old dog can't learn new tricks?" Jennifer and Sam both laughed.

hot spots and social media

"I'm so glad you brought this up today, Jen. I'm fascinated by social media. I even hired an expert to spend a few hours showing me how the various tools work and some of the best ways to use them."

"Do you think there's any way I should be incorporating these tools into my referral strategy, Sam?"

"Yes. First of all, I suggest you use the business tools first. The main ones out there now are LinkedIn and Plaxo. Some people use Facebook and Twitter for business, but that's another conversation."

"While we're talking about social media, Sam, one of my pet peeves is when people have incomplete or sloppy profile pages. I looked up one of my contacts on LinkedIn yesterday and his page didn't even say what his company does or describe the market they service. Others look like resumes—dry ones at that. It's just boring."

"You bring up a good point," said Sam. "Yes, your profile should include what your company does and the market you service. I want to stress one more thing that many people leave out: the benefits—what people and companies get from working with you. Be sure your profile includes the benefits and that it sells the feeling."

"Good point, Sam."

"Also, if you're going to use social media, I think you should be proactive. I suggest you go through your database and select the people you want to become part of your contact network. Then go to your social media site and invite all of them to connect. And don't forget to add the new people that you meet. When someone gives you a business card, consider inviting him or her to connect."

Jennifer asked, "Once I've built up my list of connections, how can I use social media as a part of my referral strategy?"

"You can do all sorts of things, Jen. I'm just beginning to scratch the surface, myself. But there is one thing that can be a powerful tie-in to your referral strategy."

"What's that?"

171

the referral code

"When you're getting ready to have the referral conversation with someone, look at his profile to see who he knows. Most social media sites allow you to go to your connections' profile page and bring up a list of the people they're connected with. In other words, you can check out your connections' connections. This is a potential treasure trove."

Sam continued, "Let's say you're going to talk with Jack about referrals and you're connected with him through one of the social media sites. You look up Jack and click through to see his connections. Make a note of anyone you may want to meet. When you talk with Jack, you can suggest that you would like an introduction to that person."

"That sounds really powerful, Sam, but won't some of my clients think I'm snooping on them?"

"Not at all. Social media sites are all about sharing and broadening your base of connections. Looking at someone's connections is not snooping—it's using the medium the way it was intended to be used."

"Okay, say I see that Jack is connected with someone I'd like to meet. How do I bring it up?"

"Suppose you're connected with Jack on LinkedIn. You could simply tell Jack you noticed that he is connected with Jill and ask how he knows her. This allows you to identify the nature and depth of the relationship. Jack may know Jill well, or he might not even know her personally.

"If it turns out that Jack has a good relationship with Jill, you could say, 'Jack, do you think that Jill or her company could benefit from our services?' If he says yes, you can ask him to make an introduction."

"This sounds great, Sam. Give me a minute to make some notes here."

When she was done writing, Jennifer asked, "When do you think is the right time to do this?"

"Unless you have great rapport with someone, I would advise against bringing up someone's social media contacts during the initial referral conversation—it could make your whole conversation seem contrived. I would wait until a later date—for example, at the next hot spot. In cases where your referral partner can't think of anyone the first time you ask, you could bring up his social media contacts when you follow up to see who has come to mind."

"This is really helpful, Sam. I'm going to take your advice on this."

"Now that these kinds of tools and information are out there, I think it would be foolish not to take advantage of them. You're already asking people who they know. Why not suggest specific people or companies that may be right for you? By researching the social media sites and suggesting people they already know, you can help them **think**. Then they can help you **link**."

"This opens up a lot of possibilities, Sam."

"Then I suggest you connect with your potential referral partners on the social media sites and look through their connections before you have a referral conversation with them. It's a no-brainer."

When to Go Off-Script

"Sam, I have another question about instincts. There have been times when it has felt awkward for me to use the state-evoker and referral questions you taught me. For example, I had lunch with a good friend yesterday. We go way back and we talk to each other about everything. With her, I feel I don't need to go through the formalized process. I could just say, 'Hey, how about giving me some referrals?'"

"Go with your instincts on the informality," said Sam. "Obviously, you don't have to be as formal with people you know really well and have great rapport with. However, no matter what the situation is, I think you should always follow a couple of guidelines: First, be sure the person is in a state of appreciation. Second, always ask an open-ended question that requires a specific response. Rather than saying, 'Hey, give me some referrals,' ask, 'Who do you know that I can help?'"

"Okay, Sam. Do you have any assignments for me this week?"

"No," said Sam. "I think you have a good handle on your referral strategy. Just stay on top of your Referral Matrix. Keep it fresh, add to it, and use it! And remember the nature of the game. Track your numbers and measure them against your objectives. At least once a year, review and refresh your referral objectives."

Jennifer asked the next question timidly, "Is this the end of our coaching?"

"Our objective was for you to learn and master a warm lead-generating system. You have certainly learned it, and by the looks of your results, you are well on your way to mastering it. Do you feel you've accomplished what you set out to do with me?"

"Yes, I do," said Jennifer. She fought back a tear, knowing that this phase of their relationship was concluding. "But what if I need some coaching along the way? I imagine I'll run across some situations where I could use your advice."

"Jen, you are not just my client; you're a dear friend. You know where to find me. I suggest we get together when it's time to review and refresh your referral objectives. We can do that in about six months."

"That would be great, Sam."

"Oh, before I forget, Jen, I have something for you." Sam reached into his shirt pocket and handed her a folded piece of paper. Puzzled, Jennifer unfolded it. It was the check she had written to Corky Starr's campaign as security that she would participate fully in the coaching commitment with Sam.

Jennifer chuckled. She tore up the check, got up, and gave Sam a hug.

"I can't find the words to express my gratitude for what you've done for me, Sam. I'll always remember it."

"It has been my sincere pleasure, Jen. I've really enjoyed watching you and your business grow. By the way, I'd like to have a little graduation celebration this Saturday night. Are you and Neil free?"

"That would be lovely, Sam. Yes, we are free."

"Great, I'll call you tonight with the details."

"By the way, Sam, we completed the technical analysis for your friend, Glenn Meyers. That was a great referral! Thanks so much."

"That's wonderful, Jen. I'm glad for you—and for Glenn."

Without missing a beat, Jennifer smiled and asked, "Sam, I was wondering, who else do you know...?"

hallelujah!

When Jennifer returned to her office, she received a call from the CEO's executive assistant.

"Hi Jennifer. Mr. Dillenberg wants to see you. Can you meet him in his office this afternoon at two?"

Jennifer was excited and a little nervous. *What does he want? Is he going to put me on the spot? What do I say if he asks me about Roger's cold-calling initiative? Do I tell him I think it was a waste of time?*

That afternoon, Jennifer met the CEO in his office. "Good afternoon, Mr. Dillenberg."

"Hi Jennifer. Please, call me Kenny."

"Okay, Kenny."

"Well, Jennifer, Roger tells me you've done some pretty impressive work over the past couple of months. He says you've used referrals to open up nine new prospects in 60 days and five have turned into RFPs. And you closed one of our most detailed technical analysis meetings. That's quite a batting average, especially in this economy."

"Thanks, Kenny. That's the power of the warm-lead generating system I've been using. By the way, the referrals I have been getting are all qualified leads."

"With that kind of success rate, they must be."

the referral code

"Also, I don't know if Roger told you that I'm about to meet with Yang Enterprises. Based on what I know so far, the account could represent as much as $15 million over the next two years, not to mention where it could go from there."

"Yes, I'm well aware of that. Great work, Jennifer! How did you do generate all this activity in such a short time?"

"There's a lot to it, but in a nutshell, I tapped into my existing relationships and asked for referrals."

"Roger tells me you've been using some sort of a referral system or strategy. I'd like to know more about it and where it came from."

Jennifer replied, "I'm not sure where to begin."

"How about at the beginning?" Kenny, sat back, put his hands behind his head, and gave Jennifer the floor.

Jennifer's nervousness melted away. Something about Kenny's tone of voice and body language made her feel at-ease and free to open up.

Jennifer began, "My husband, Neil, is in the financial services business. A couple years ago, he met a man named Sam Martin, who coached him out of a sales slump to become his company's top producer. Sam says that people buy based on feelings. He wrote a book about his approach; it's called *Sell the Feeling*. Neil and Sam became fast friends, and when Neil and I got together, Sam became my friend too.

"When the economy took a nosedive last year, my business started to dry up. A number of my clients took their IT services in-house or scaled back on our services. As you know, a few others either went out of business or were acquired by other companies."

Kenny replied, "I'm well aware."

Jennifer continued, "I realized that I would have to do something different to replace the lost business and generate new clients in the down market. Neil recommended I call Sam to see if he had any suggestions. Sam and I met and he agreed to coach me."

Kenny replied, "I salute you for hiring a coach. It's a great investment in yourself. I just started working with an executive coach to assist me in turning the company around. So far, the experience has been eye-opening and challenging. It's forcing me to think outside the box and take certain actions that have been outside my comfort zone."

"Same with me, Kenny."

"Back to your story, Jennifer, what did you learn from Sam?"

"Sam has taught me a lot about relationships. He showed me that my existing relationships carry the seeds of future business. He says that warm beats cold every time."

"What do you mean by that?"

"Warm leads from people that love you are much more likely to bear fruit than any cold-calling system."

"Love? What does that have to do with business?"

"Actually, a lot. Sam has this saying: There are people that love you and love the work you do, and they have people that they love and love them too, that need to love you."

Kenny burst out laughing. "That's clever, but come on—we're selling business-to-business solutions. What's love got to do with that?"

Jennifer pressed on, "If love is too touchy-feely for you, call it respect, admiration, or long-term trust. Kenny, I know you may be thinking this love thing sounds airy-fairy, and frankly, so did I when Sam first talked to me about it. But I've seen it work, I've shown it works, and I've become a believer."

"A believer, eh?" Kenny gave Jennifer an impish grin and raised his hands into the air. "Hallelujah!"

Jennifer smiled, raised her hands, and repeated, "Hallelujah!" They both laughed. Jennifer thought, *We've got rapport!*

Jennifer continued, "Sam taught me about the value of the goodwill I've created in my relationships. I'll never forget what he said to me one day: 'Goodwill is the emotional currency of business relationships.'"

Kenny smiled. "I can see that business relationships are based on a foundation of trust and goodwill. Once you have this goodwill, how do you use it to get referrals?"

Jennifer responded, "Basically, you go to the people with whom you've created goodwill and ask them for referrals. But the key is **when** and **how** you ask."

"Okay, I'll bite. When and how do you ask?"

"People are much more likely to give you referrals when they are in a state of appreciation." Jennifer told Kenny the story about Sam's granddaughter asking for two cookies.

Kenny responded, "It makes perfect sense—people are more apt to give you what you want when they feel good about you. It's human nature. How do you get them into that state of appreciation?"

"Sometimes they go into it naturally, like when they express appreciation for a job well-done. But instead of relying on the circumstances, Sam taught me how to deliberately evoke a state of appreciation."

Jennifer told Kenny about the state-evoker question: What are some of the things that have worked for you in our working together?

Then she told him about the referral question: Who do you know that can benefit from some of the same things you described...? As she told Kenny about the rest of the referral process, she noticed that he was nodding.

Then she told him about the Referral Matrix and how she had planned, executed, and paced her referral strategy over the past two months.

hallelujah!

When she was done, Kenny said, "Thanks, Jennifer. This is intriguing. I certainly see your point that it is a good idea to ask for referrals proactively. I've known a lot of salespeople in my time. Many of them say they get most of their business through referrals, but I don't think many of them ask proactively, and I have never heard of anyone doing it the way you talked about. And I can only think of handful of times when anyone has come right out and asked me for referrals. Why do you think that is?"

"That's a great question, Kenny. Sam says it is because they are afraid to ask, and I agree." Jennifer told Kenny about the Three Ugly Sisters: the fear of being seen as pushy, the fear of being perceived as needy, and the fear of being rejected.

Kenny responded, "I can relate. I remember selling chocolate bars door-to-door for my church youth group way back when. I experienced those fears every time I knocked on someone's door."

Jennifer replied, "I think most salespeople who call on people have these fears at one time or another—they're universal."

"Jennifer, I have one more question for you. Don't people expect something in return for helping you, like some kind of a fee or a referral in return? And doesn't that put you in an awkward position sometimes?"

"That's what I thought too, but Sam has a great take on this. Once you've created goodwill, people are more than willing to give you referrals. It's not so much about helping you—it's about paying it forward to the people they care about. Plus they get to feel like a hero for passing on a good thing."

"I like everything you are telling me today, Jennifer. I want to think this all over and digest it. Maybe we can introduce this system to our sales team. Your coach Sam seems like a sharp guy. I'd like to talk with him someday."

Kenny looked at his watch. "I've got to head out to my next meeting now. Thanks for enlightening me about your referral strategy, and congratulations on a job well-done. I am looking forward to more great things from you."

"Thanks for your interest, Kenny. I assume it's alright with you if I continue to focus my efforts on the referral strategy."

the referral code

"Of course, Jennifer, as long as it's working."

Jennifer left Kenny's office in the executive suite and walked down the hallway back to her office.

She remembered storming down the same hall six months earlier, infuriated over Needleman's pep talk in which he announced his cold-calling mandate. She remembered how intensely she disliked him.

Much water had passed under the bridge since then. She was now grateful for the challenge that had been placed in her path. Without it, she might never have learned the Referral Code. Now she was heading in a new upward trajectory in her business and Needleman was on the way out. If it weren't for Old Needlenose, she wouldn't be where she was now.

She chuckled to herself and thought, *What a strange twist of fate. It's amazing how the world works sometimes.*

sam's story

Sam invited Jennifer and Neil to an exotic Moroccan restaurant to celebrate Jennifer's recent success. He had arranged for a corner table in a small dining room appointed with brightly colored throw rugs and wall tapestries. They sat on the floor on lush pillows and watched as belly dancers swirled and twirled to Moroccan music. The meal was a sumptuous seven-course feast, which Sam had ordered in advance.

The mood was joyous and the wine flowed freely. Jennifer and Neil had never been to a Moroccan restaurant, and they loved the food and the experience.

Sam and Neil both toasted Jennifer, and she reveled in the attention. Jennifer toasted Sam for all he had done for her and Neil for his ongoing love and support.

After the toasts, Jennifer replenished their glasses and said, "I have something for you, Sam." She handed him a beautifully wrapped gift.

When Sam unwrapped it, his eyes widened and his jaw dropped. Speechless, he held the gift up for all to see. It was a framed original cartoon from 1932 showing Babe Ruth pointing to the centerfield fence in Wrigley Field. It was a depiction of 'the called shot' that the owner of the sports bar had described to Jennifer the day that Sam taught her about the nature of the game.

"This is going on my wall tomorrow. Thanks so much, Jen. I will cherish this, not just because I'm a diehard Yankees' fan, but also because it reminds me of our relationship and the time we spent together. Now this is what I call a classy gift." Sam and Jennifer gave each other a knowing look, recalling their conversation about gifts.

the referral code

Between the third and fourth course, Jennifer turned to Sam and said, "You know, I've never asked you about the origins of the Referral Code. Where did it come from?"

Sam adjusted his pillows and made himself more comfortable. He took a sip of wine and began.

"As you and Neil have probably noticed, I'm a big believer in systems. When it comes to sales and influence, which are my passions, I've always looked for systematic ways to do things better. I like to draw on diverse experiences and sources. I'm also passionate about empowering people to build mutually beneficial connections. It's my way of leaving the world a little better.

"It all began when I was a young rookie selling life insurance back in Texas. The company sent us to New Jersey for a month-long training program. In the training, they placed a big emphasis on us getting referrals from clients. They had a referral system that they drilled into us. When we met with a prospective client, we would gather the prospect's information and schedule an appointment to deliver a family financial analysis report and our recommendations for insurance coverage.

"I'll never forget what they told us to say at the end of the first meeting: 'Mr. Prospect, before we conclude, I think it's important that you know how I get paid. I do not get paid to meet with you or to create the personal financial report. I actually get paid very little when you buy a policy from me. The way I get paid is by referrals to your family and friends. At the end of this process, I think you will find that I have provided an extremely valuable service. If so, I would like the opportunity to meet with other people you know—good people like you. When I deliver the policy for your signature, I am going to ask you to open up your address book and give me the names of people that you care about who deserve the same kind of excellent service and protection that I have provided to you.'"

Jennifer rolled her eyes, "Why on earth would a prospect care about how the insurance agent gets paid?"

Sam responded, "Exactly! That conversation is focused on the salesperson's needs, not the client's need. Plus, they wanted us to start talking about referrals before we had delivered any real value. It was all bass-ackwards. And believe it or not, the company is still using that same script."

Neil added, "That script could be a great way to break rapport!" Sam and Jennifer nodded in agreement.

Sam continued his story, "Being a newbie, I used the company's referral script for the first year or so that I was in the business. Sometimes it worked, and I would get a name or two. But when I called my clients' family or friends, more times than not, they weren't interested in meeting with me. In other words, I was spending my time chasing unqualified referrals. I began to dread asking for referrals. When I refer to the Three Ugly Sisters, I know what I'm talking about—I've had plenty of personal experience feeling pushy, needy, and rejected.

"I finally figured it out and changed my strategy. I started waiting until I delivered the policy—until we had had time to get to know each other better—to ask my clients for referrals.

"Because of my early experiences feeling pushy, needy and rejected, I softened my script. I would say, "Mr. Prospect, it has been a pleasure getting to know you, and I am certain that you will feel happy and secure knowing you've done the right thing to protect your family. Please keep my card handy and if you know any good people who want to protect their families, please don't hesitate to contact me. You can be sure I will treat your referrals with the same kid-glove care I've given you."

Jennifer remarked, "That's the old if-then question we talked about when we first got together."

"You're right, Jen. And as I told you then, it's better than nothing. I felt more comfortable than I did with the company's script, and I was a bit more successful in getting referrals, but not much.

"Around that time, I met a house painter named Woody at a local Rotary Club and we became friends. Woody had one of those larger-than-life personalities. Everybody loved Woody.

"Sometimes Woody would get right in my face and say, 'Come on, Sammy boy! Ya' gotta bring me some business. Come on, man! Who do you know? Everyone has a house. Everyone needs their house painted. Who do you know? Who do you know?'

"Finally, I gave him the name of a friend. He said, 'Thanks, Sammy boy! Anyone else? Who else do you know?'

"He kept at me until I gave him four or five names. I saw him do the same thing with a couple other people. Woody was getting a bucket load of referrals—a lot more than I was.

"I started thinking about it. I analyzed my way of asking and his. My way of asking wasn't even a question. 'If you know anyone, then please don't hesitate to contact me.' It was a statement, so it didn't call for an answer. Woody came right out and said, 'Who do you know?' People had to answer, and that's why it worked.

"Now of course, Woody didn't have professional behavior. He came on too strong and too needy—he made it all about helping him. But there was something about his direct question that presumed a response—in this case, not a yes or a no, but a name.

"I decided to model Woody's language, so I came up with 'Who do you know that could use my services?' As soon as I started asking a question that prompted a specific kind of response, more people started giving me referrals.

"Around this time, I became aware of how important a buyer's emotional state is in selling. It seemed to me that getting referrals was a form of selling—in this case, selling someone on the idea of referring me business. I asked myself what state someone would need to be in order to feel motivated to give me referrals.

"One day I met with a client to deliver his life insurance policy. At one point in the meeting he said to me, 'Sam, I've got to tell you how much I appreciate the time and care you have taken to get to know me and make sure that I got the right policy for my needs. I feel really good about working with you.' Something told me that it was the perfect time to ask him for referrals, which I did. He said he would be happy to refer me, and right then he started looking through his

Rolodex. He came up with several referrals and started calling them to tell them about me, all while I was there in his office. I was amazed—no one had ever been that proactive about referring me.

"Later, I tried to analyze what had gone so right. I realized that I had asked him for referrals right after he told me he appreciated me and my work. That was it—appreciation was the ideal state! From then on, I made it a point to ask for referrals when a client expressed appreciation. As a result, I started getting more referrals.

"The problem was that I had to wait until someone was in a state of appreciation before I could ask for referrals. I wondered how could I evoke that state, so that I could ask for referrals whenever I wanted. I couldn't just ask someone if they appreciated me. I needed to come up with a way to do it in a professional manner that didn't seem like I was fishing for a compliment. After much thought and practice, I arrived at the state-evoker question: What are some of the things that have worked for you in our working together?"

Jennifer said, "This is all interesting, Sam. One of the most valuable things I got from you was getting over the feeling of being needy. How did you come up with the idea that asking referrals isn't about asking for help?"

"Good question. One day I delivered an insurance policy to a client and had my referral conversation with him. He told me he was satisfied with my service and would think about people he could recommend. He called me the next week and gave me the names of seven of his friends. I had never received that many referrals at once. I was stunned and grateful. I remember saying to him, 'Thank you so much. I really appreciate your helping me!'

"He was a tough old coot—the kind of person who said exactly what was on his mind." Sam recounted the conversation, using his best gravely voice and Texas accent. "'Son, I could give a horse's hindquarters about helping **you!** You ain't my friend, nor my kin. But I **do** care about my friends and their families, and they need insurance. Some day, when they pass on, their families will thank me—if I'm still kicking.'"

the referral code

Jennifer and Neil laughed and refilled Sam's wine glass. They were clearly enjoying his stories.

Sam continued, "That's when it dawned on me. It's a mistake to assume that someone's motivation to refer you business is to help **you**. It may be the case some of the time, but it misses the larger point: people refer you to pass on a good thing to those they care about—in other words, to pay it forward. Plus, they get to be the hero. I'm not saying that people don't want to help you. But if you go into a referral conversation looking for help, you will be coming from a position of neediness, which will show up in your words, your tone, or your state."

Jennifer replied, "That is so true. Once I got that it's not about me, my referral conversations became a lot easier."

Neil jumped in, "Sam, Jennifer told me what you said about love. There are people that love you and they love other people who ought to be loving you? Is that it?"

Sam chuckled. "Not exactly. It goes like this: There are people who love you and love the work you do, that have people they love that love them too, who need to love you."

Neil replied, "I love it! How did you come up with that, Sam?"

"It's an interesting story. Do you remember when I told you about my friend and mentor, Carlos?"

"I think so," said Neil. "We talked about him when you coached me. He was your coach and spiritual guru, right?"

"I wouldn't call him a spiritual guru, but he certainly talked about spiritual matters. And yes, he did coach me every week on the phone for nearly four years. I met Carlos in Colorado on a backpacking trip almost 15 years ago. He was a wise and gifted man.

"One day, I received a letter from Carlos. He told me he had been diagnosed with a terminal illness and had perhaps a year to live. He said he was at peace with it. He was writing to invite me to a celebration of his life at a mountain retreat in Colorado. The celebration was three days long. Of course, I had to go.

"I flew into Denver, rented a car, and drove a couple hours to a beautiful lodge nestled in the mountains. It was late spring and the mountaintops were topped with snow. The area was surrounded by gorgeous lakes, Aspen trees, and hot springs. It was breathtaking.

"Carlos was a special man, and he touched many people in a profound way. He invited about 150 of his closest friends and relatives to the celebration. People flew in from all over the U.S. and several other countries.

"I'll always remember the welcome speech he gave the first night before dinner. He thanked us all for coming, talked about the gift of life, and said what a pleasure and honor it was to know all of us. The room was filled with love and admiration for this great man.

"At the end of his speech, he said something I will never forget: 'Take a look around. Look to your left and to your right. Look in front and behind you. This room is filled with magnificent, wonderful people. One of the main reasons I called you all here is that I want you to know each other. Nothing would give me greater satisfaction to leave this dimension of time and space knowing that I have left a legacy of relationships between the people gathered here tonight. I love every one of you, and now you need to love each other.'"

Sam paused and wiped a tear from his eye, then said, "There wasn't a dry eye in the house." Sam, Jennifer, and Neil looked at each other. There wasn't a dry eye at their table either.

As he recalled Carlos, Sam closed his eyes for a moment. He took a sip of wine and continued, "I thought a lot about what Carlos said that night, especially the part about 'I love every one of you and now you need to love each other.' It was a beautiful sentiment and it really made an impression on me about the value of connections between people.

"It didn't take me long to realize that the same principle could apply to giving and receiving business referrals. That's how I came up with my phrase: There are people who love you and love the work you do that have people they love that love them too, who need to love you.

the referral code

"Back to my story—Carlos arranged a spectacular weekend, all designed for us to get to know each other. We went on group hikes and river rafting trips, and we shared communal meals in the lodge. By the end of the weekend, we had all made new friendships.

"At the closing dinner, Carlos thanked us all for coming and for being a part of his life. He said, 'I've lived a rich and wonderful life. As I get ready to depart, there's one thought I want leave you with: the most valuable thing in this life is our relationships. Sometimes, in the face of problems or in our obsession to make money, we lose sight of that. Be grateful for your relationships, nurture them, and make new ones. Your potential for creating and receiving value is infinite, and it all starts and ends with relationships. I urge you all to reach out and connect with your relationships and connect them to each other. Connect, connect, connect!'"

Your potential for creating and receiving value is infinite, and it all starts and ends with relationships.

⟶

After a few moments, Jennifer spoke, "That's a great story, Sam. So what happened next?"

"Those of us who attended the celebration were so moved that we decided to preserve his legacy. We formed a society called Friends of Carlos and agreed to spend a group weekend at some beautiful vacation spot every two years.

"Soon after the retreat, Carlos became quite sick. I visited him one last time and talked to him about Friends of Carlos and our plans to stay in touch and meet periodically. By that time, he was very weak and could barely talk. He gave me a smile and took my hand. I could tell he was very happy about our plans. He died a couple weeks later.

"It's been 12 years since he died and the Friends of Carlos society is still going strong. We've kept our promise to meet every couple of years. Many of us bring new people into the group to continue the legacy. The weekend retreat that Carlos planned has been a blessing. The relationships we have formed since then have led to all sorts of wonderful things, including business ventures and referrals, charitable foundations, and even a couple of marriages."

Neil said, "Sounds like a great group. Is there any way we can get involved?"

"I'll invite you to our retreat next year."

Jennifer replied, "Thanks, Sam."

Sam added, "I must say that much of my passion and motivation for teaching this referral system comes from what I learned from Carlos."

Jennifer replenished the wine in all three glasses then proposed a toast, "To Carlos—his legacy lives on!"

After the toast, Sam continued, "I know I've been talking a long time, but there's more to this story, if I may."

Neil said, "By all means, keep going."

"Like I said, we've formed some great relationships though Friends of Carlos. I've had a couple tremendous business opportunities that came from people in the group. As a result of one of my relationships, every year I travel to a different state and spend a couple weeks building houses for poor people. It not only helps them, but I get deep satisfaction from it. My working on this project is a direct result of Carlos' legacy."

Sam continued, "As you know, I recently took a rafting expedition down the Colorado River. My fellow travelers were people I know through Friends of Carlos. One night I got to talking with a guy named Henry. He told me that his sister had been recently diagnosed with a rare form of leukemia and she was not expected to live through the end of the year.

"It just so happens that I'm good friends with a doctor in San Francisco who has developed some experimental protocols for treating leukemia. One of the guys on the trip had a satellite phone, so I used it to call my friend. Later that week, we got word that Henry's sister had flown to San Francisco to meet him. Turns out that she was a perfect candidate for his study. She is now receiving treatment. It's experimental, and no one knows whether it will make a difference, but it could. She and her family have renewed hope. The point is: this possibility was created through relationships.

the referral code

"After my conversation with Henry, I started thinking about the potential connections between people. That evening, I lay on the ground and gazed at the stars for a couple of hours. As I looked into the infinity of space, I contemplated the infinite possibilities of connections between people and potential value that could be created in all areas of human endeavor as a result of these connections.

"I saw that just about every good thing that had ever come into my life was a result of some connection or relationship. I met my late wife though a friend from college. I got started in business years ago because of a connection I made through my dad. I decided to develop the *Sell the Feeling* book and workshops largely as a result of my work with Neil. And without my existing friendship with Neil, I wouldn't have had the good fortune of knowing and working with you, Jennifer."

Sam raised his glass in Jennifer's direction to salute her. "And as a result of the work we've done together, both of you will no doubt reach new clients and customers and help them. And on and on and on.

"Anyway, that night under the stars, I realized that just about everything of value that people create in this world somehow springs from their connections with others. And there's a multiplication factor. Carlos not only helped change my life for the better, he also introduced me to others who have made a huge difference for me. And because of the connections we've made in the Friends of Carlos, we have made a difference for others, such as those who are living in the houses we've built. That night I really grasped what Carlos meant when he said, 'Connect, connect, connect!'

Who knows what possibilities may be only a phone call or a meeting or a relationship or two away?

➡

"You know, sometimes as we go about the business of our daily lives, caught up in whatever we're doing or consumed in our problems or struggles, we're blinded to the infinite field of possibilities and opportunities that lay before us. Who knows what possibilities may be only a phone call or a meeting or a relationship or two away?"

sam's story

Sam paused and took a sip of wine, "I hope I'm not getting too esoteric for you."

Jennifer said "No, not at all," and Neil agreed.

Sam continued, "I like to imagine that there's an invisible web connecting us all to one another, kind of like a gossamer telephone network. We may need to meet certain people at different times in our lives. Consciously or unconsciously, we send out signals. Sometimes the signals travel along the web, and the right person just shows up at the right time. It seems like luck, or magic, or something that was meant to be. It's as if the universe is giving us exactly what we need.

"It pays to be to be alert, open, and receptive to people. If we're closed off or cynical, we may miss opportunities to make useful or valuable connections with others. You never know who might give you a referral or connect you to an opportunity.

"A woman I coach travels frequently to meet with clients and prospects. She intensely dislikes talking with strangers on the plane and does all she can to avoid in-flight conversations. She actually told me, 'I'm a bitch on planes.'

"One day she's on a flight with her head buried in a book. The guy next to her starts talking to her. She tries to ignore him, but he's persistent. He asks her what she does, and she tells him she sells employee benefits packages to large companies. He keeps asking her questions, and she keeps trying to end the conversation. Finally, she asks what he does. It turns out he's the CEO of a large company, and he's headed to a company meeting to discuss, among other things, employee benefits. By the time the plane landed, she had secured a meeting with him, the CFO, and the head of HR.

"She said to me, 'That experience really opened my eyes. Who knows how many opportunities I may have missed in the past by being so closed off. My bitch days are over.'"

"That's a great story, Sam," said Neil. "How do you think that happened?"

"I don't know. Maybe it was a fluke. Maybe the 'invisible web' got activated. Maybe it was one of those times that the universe taps someone on the shoulder and says, 'Wake up.'"

Jennifer asked Sam, "Do you believe in the Law of Attraction?"

Sam responded, "There's a lot of talk about the Law of Attraction these days. They say focus clearly on your intention and you will attract it. There's some truth to this, but in my opinion, a couple of big pieces are missing. One is that you must do the work. And the more focused, intentional, and targeted the work is, the better your chances are of getting what you are after. That's what the Referral Code system I've taught you is all about.

"Besides your intentions and the work, there's another crucial element to this business of attraction: your beliefs. What you believe deep down about yourself, your goals, the world, and other people can make or break your chances of success. Our beliefs drive our actions, and therefore, our results. The universe eavesdrops on our beliefs and attracts situations or opportunities to us, waiting for our attention, reception, and response.

The universe eavesdrops on our beliefs and attracts situations or opportunities to us, waiting for our attention, reception, and response.

➡

"Some people say they want something, but deep down, they have limiting beliefs that contradict their getting it. For example, some people believe they're not good enough, not deserving, or that people will screw them—something negative like that. No matter how intent you are, no matter how hard you work, if you have a limiting belief, it will somehow manifest. Beliefs are invitations to the universe to give us a hand that will either support us or slap us—it all depends on whether your beliefs are expansive or limiting."

Jennifer remarked, "Kind of like the beliefs I had about being pushy, needy, and rejected?"

"Right, those were limiting beliefs wrapped in fear," said Sam. "Do you notice that once we dispelled those beliefs, your fears disappeared?"

Jennifer responded, "Yes, as a matter of fact now that you mention it, the fears are gone. I no longer have any hesitation in asking for referrals."

"Good! I want to say some more about the importance of doing the work. Many people think they should get referrals because they're good at what they do. Sure, by being competent, serving your clients well, and creating goodwill, you will probably attract some referrals organically. But it's been my experience that no matter how good you are, and how good your relationships are, the organic way will only take you so far. To tap into the true potential of your relationships to bring you more business, you've got to buckle down and do the work. The work is the planning, the asking, and the follow up—everything that I've taught you. To do it well— to reap the benefits over time—you need to make it an ongoing never-ending practice. The potential rewards are great and the possibilities are endless—that is, unless you believe otherwise."

Beliefs are invitations to the universe to give us a hand that will either support us or slap us—it all depends on whether your beliefs are expansive or limiting.

"Well put!" Neil said. They all took another sip of wine.

Jennifer noticed a buzzing and reached into her purse and took out her phone. She looked at the message that had just arrived and exclaimed, "Oh, my God!"

Neil asked, "What is it—is everything okay?"

Jennifer said, "You're not going to believe this. It's from Kenny Dillenberg, the CEO of my company."

Jennifer showed the message to Neil and Sam:

the referral code

Been thinking about our discussion. Please send me Sam's
contact info. I want to talk to him about training the dept.

Neil gasped, "Talk about timing!"

Sam smiled and said, "Great! I'd be happy to talk with your CEO. Why don't you go ahead and give him my number. And of course, thanks. I appreciate your telling him about me."

Jennifer emailed Sam's contact information to Kenny.

"There's one more piece to my story," Sam continued. "While I was on the rafting trip, I got to talking with one of my friends about my coaching and training business. He told me he might have a good referral for me: a business owner named Lydia Cooke. When I got back to town, I called her, and we arranged to meet. We talked business for a while, then moved onto other things. We really hit it off. We decided to continue talking over dinner. By the end of the evening, I was smitten, and so was she. We've been seeing each other ever since. It's been less than two months, but between the three of us, I think she's The One!"

Jennifer cried out, "Oh My God, Sam! How wonderful!"

Neil echoed, "That's great, Sam!"

They raised their glasses and toasted Sam and Lydia.

Before they had time to put their glasses down, Jennifer exclaimed, "Sam!"

"What?"

"You've spent the last six months teaching me to turn relationships into referrals, but now you've turned a referral into a relationship!"

Sam chuckled and gave a wry smile, "Well, romance aside, we should all look forward to turning referrals into relationships, then turning those relationships into more referrals, wouldn't you agree?"

Chapter 27

epilogue (nine months later)

Sitting at her desk, Jennifer felt a profound sense of gratitude for the wonderful opportunities and growth she had experienced since she began working with Sam over a year ago. Then she noticed the unopened envelope in her inbox. It was a letter from Roger Needleman.

Well I'll be damned, she thought, as she reached for the letter.

Nine months earlier, Jennifer received the company-wide email announcing that Roger had 'resigned' his position. After her meeting with Roger—the one where he confided to her that he was leaving—she never saw him again. He didn't say good-bye to anyone in the sales division and left no contact information.

Since Roger's departure, Jennifer often thought about him and wondered where and how he was. Despite all she didn't like about him, she knew he had given her a golden opportunity to prove herself. And in the face of his own termination, he had selflessly praised her to the CEO, Kenny Dillenberg.

That conversation set off a chain of events: Kenny met with Jennifer and she told him about Sam. Kenny brought Sam in to teach the Referral Code system to the sales team and the new VP of Sales.

At the end of the referral training, Sam told the team, "Now you know what to do to bring in a constant stream of business. Many of you have told me that you think this is a great system and are excited to launch into it. I appreciate your enthusiasm.

"Here's the reality of the situation: Some of you will put what you've just learned into practice and you will reap rewards. Then there are those of you who have great intentions, but will procrastinate and ultimately fail to take action. Instead you will keep doing whatever you were already doing and continue to get pretty much the same results."

Sam concluded the training by saying, "Please hear this: The Referral Code **will** work for you, but only if **you** work it. The question is: If not you, who, and if not now, when? The reality is: the choice is yours and the time is now."

> *The Referral Code* **will** *work for you, but only* if **you** *work it. The* *choice is yours and the* *time is now.*
>
> ➜

The account managers who took on the Referral Code began to generate more qualified referrals, culminating in additional sales. Largely due to their production, the company's gross sales increased 32 percent in six months. Despite the still-teetering economy, Pacific IT Solutions was moving back to financial health.

When Jennifer thought about Roger, she often marveled at the irony of the situation. The person she had once seen as her greatest obstacle had inadvertently provided her an opportunity for growth and advancement.

Jennifer opened Roger's letter and began reading.

Dear Jennifer,

I've been meaning to write you for a long time. I apologize for disappearing without saying good-bye. To tell you the truth, I just didn't feel up to facing anyone once I received my marching orders. I know I wasn't very popular with the troops and that almost everyone hated my cold-calling program (and maybe even my guts).

When I left, not only did I feel a sense of personal failure, I also felt I had let the company and the sales division down. How ironic that I was the one who wasn't around to attend the company Christmas party.

epilogue (nine months later)

I am writing to thank you. Let me explain.

When I left PITS, I took a couple months off to lick my wounds. Then I hired an executive headhunter to help me find another position. Because of the economy, the job market was pretty thin. I waited for the phone to ring, but nothing came up. I twiddled my thumbs and moped around the house for a couple months.

Last October, I took a hunting trip. I was in a duck blind at 5 in the morning, when it occurred to me: why not use some of Jennifer's referral techniques to look for work.

When I got home, I went through my database and business cards, and recalling what you shared with me, I put together my own referral matrix. I started reconnecting with my business and industry contacts, using many of your methodologies. I asked them who they knew that could benefit from my skills and experience. A number of them introduced me to their connections immediately. Within a few weeks, I had several interviews lined up.

I wound up taking a job as Regional Sales Director at a human resource outsourcing company called The Rose Group in Houston. Upon starting, I decided to implement your referral program, as I remembered it, with my team of account executives. Long story short, it's been a huge success. My division's sales are up 18% since I came on board five months ago.

Jennifer, I owe you and Sam (who I never had the good fortune to meet) a debt of gratitude. If it weren't for you and your Referral Code, I wouldn't be in the position that I'm in now. I daresay I'm considered a bit of a hero here.

the referral code

I look forward to learning more about the Referral Code. I'm thinking of getting in touch with Sam. Will you please send me his contact info?

By the way, as far as I know, no one here calls me 'Old Needlenose' (yes, I was listening).

Please stay in touch. I wish you all the best.

Fondly,
Roger

When Jennifer showed the letter to Neil, he said, "I guess an old dog **can** learn new tricks."

In the 12 months since she had implemented the Referral Code, Jennifer had became the company's top producer. She had increased not only her book of business, but her pipeline as well. For various reasons, some of the prospects she met with had not signed up to do business with PITS, but were definitely interested in talking in the future. Jennifer kept them on her follow-up list. She kept in mind what Sam said: "Delays are not denials."

Jennifer's biggest homerun for the year was the worldwide electronics distribution company, Yang Enterprises, a referral from her client Hans. After several meetings and a detailed technical analysis, Jennifer signed Yang to a two-year multi-site contract worth $15 million.

Jennifer knew that this was only the beginning of the relationship with Yang. The company was growing and had plans to expand into the Pacific Northwest and Canada. Besides the possibility for more business within Yang, Jennifer knew that once the relationship became more solid, Ravi Singh, Yang's Data Center director, could become a great referral source, especially within the electronics industry.

epilogue (nine months later)

Jennifer saw her Referral Matrix as the master document of her business development plan. She kept it in front of her at all times, continually updating it with new relationships, while monitoring her current ones.

Once she had a referral conversation with someone, she stayed on the lookout for hot spots as opportunities to ask for more referrals. Sometimes she didn't have to go to the well again—a number of her clients began volunteering referrals, weeks, or even months, after their referral conversation.

As Jennifer continued to fill her pipeline, she often wondered what new connections were in store for her. She was excited by the possibility of building more and more relationships over time.

Jennifer had come a long way, not only in her business, but also in her mindset. Though the economy was still shaky, she saw a bright future ahead. If the economy stumbled again, she knew she would always reach out to her relationships and create new opportunities.

Jennifer was grateful for her relationship with Sam. She realized she would never have gotten to this point without being coached in the Referral Code. She had always been confident, self-sufficient, and a hard worker. But just like the rest of us, she was too close to her own situation, her own habits, and her own way of thinking, to see how she was getting in her own way and what changes were necessary to propel her to the next level.

She would continue to meet with Sam to help keep her game fresh, on-track, and in-check. Like her CEO, Kenny Dillenberg, she had become a strong advocate of coaching, training, and mentoring.

Sam was right: almost all progress and value stem from relationships. Jennifer's relationships with clients, friends, and associates had led to opportunities for her to help the people they knew. She remembered what Sam had said that night in the Moroccan restaurant:

"Your potential for creating and receiving value is infinite, and it all starts and ends with relationships."

No truer words have ever been spoken.

acknowledgements

Our heartfelt thanks to:

- Our families for their unconditional support and giving us the time and space to work on this book. Special thanks to Lisa McCullough for coming up with a brilliant title, *The Referral Code*.

- The brilliant pioneers and teachers in the field of NLP and hypnosis. Thanks especially to Dr. Tad James for your great mentoring and training.

- David, Hancock, Rick Frishman, Margo Toulouse, and everyone else at Morgan James Publishing for giving us the opportunity to take our referral system to a larger audience.

- Jocelyn Baker of Ghostwriters Anonymous, for editing and polishing our manuscript.

- Rachel Lopez for her cool cover design and Bonnie Bushman for the excellent layout of the book's interior.

- Our numerous friends, clients, and associates who gave us valuable support and feedback.

- All the remarkable (and not-so-remarkable) salespeople and professionals who inspired us to write this book.

- We want to give special thanks to our clients: We've learned as much from you as you have from us. Continue learning, teaching, and growing.

- Finally, we want to acknowledge you, our readers, for investing the time, energy to learn about the Referral Code system. Now get out there and use it!

about the authors

arry Pinci and Phil Glosserman are top business and sales trainers and coaches who work with senior executives, business owners, and sales teams throughout North America. They have earned a solid reputation for leading companies to develop the strategies, actions, and mindset needed to fuel significant sales and business growth. Their sales and referral training programs have been called 'the most eye-opening and effective' business seminars on the market today. Within in 12 months of attending these seminars, participants have seen their sales results improve up to 250%. Larry and Phil are based in Los Angeles, California.

Larry and Phil's first book, *Sell the Feeling the 6-Step System that Drives People to Do Business with You* was awarded U.S. Book News Best Business/Sales Book in 2007 and Axiom Gold Medal for Best Business Fable in 2008.

Larry Pinci is originally from Melbourne, Australia, and has been honing his unique brand of training and coaching for over 20 years. Certified as a Master Coach and Trainer of both NLP (Neuro Linguistic Programming) and Clinical Hypnotherapy, he is an accomplished mediator and a dynamic professional speaker.

Phil Glosserman has over a decade of experience as a business and sales performance coach. Before becoming a coach, he spent 14 years as a senior manager in the software industry and 10 years as a professional drummer. Phil is a certified Master Practitioner and Trainer of NLP, a certified Kolbe Practitioner, and a graduate of Corporate Coach University, International.

You can e-mail Larry and Phil at **authors@sellthefeeling.com**.

training and coaching programs

We offer onsite training and coaching programs, custom-tailored for your company and industry. Our sales and referral training programs have been called 'the most eye-opening and effective' business seminars on the market today. Within in 12 months of attending these seminars, our participants have seen their sales results improve up to 250%.

Mastering the Referral Game – In this intensive one-day workshop, your team will learn the entire Referral Code system. The seminar includes advanced techniques and tools that go way beyond the material in this book.

Sell the Feeling I – In this intensive workshop you will learn and practice the steps necessary to get inside your prospects' heads and create the feelings that lead them to do business with you. Regardless of your current experience or success, you will leave this training with a whole new power to influence your prospects, clients, and customers, and sell more effectively than you ever have.

Sell the Feeling II – This seminar builds on and goes beyond Sell the Feeling I. You team will learn the latest advances in the science of influence and suggestion.

Sell the Feeling III – This advanced workshop builds on *Sell the Feeling* I and II and shows you specific techniques to win more repeat business and create clients/customers for life.

Sell the Feeling Coaches Training – This training program teaches sales directors, managers, and assistant managers how to incorporate the *Sell the Feeling* system into their sales force and company culture. You will learn to identify the breakdowns and incorporate the needed enhancements in your team's selling game. You will learn how to coach your team and individuals to increase their sales performance significantly.

the referral code

Sell the Feeling Trainers Training – We will train your corporate trainers to teach *Sell the Feeling* and install the system into your company culture. This training includes licensing our proprietary training systems and materials.

Executive Coaching – We provide one-on-one master-level coaching for senior executives and entrepreneurs who want to take their sales and company to the next level.

Individual and Group Sales Coaching – We will create a customized coaching program to address your or your organization's specific goals and challenges. In coaching, we focus on the strategies, actions, mindset, and discipline needed to create outstanding sales results. Our program combines practical skills with advanced selling skills, and addresses the "mental game" of staying consistently motivated and in action.

For further information about our training and coaching programs, go to: **www.sellthefeeling.com**

BUY A SHARE OF THE FUTURE IN YOUR COMMUNITY

These certificates make great holiday, graduation and birthday gifts that can be personalized with the recipient's name. The cost of one S.H.A.R.E. or one square foot is $54.17. The personalized certificate is suitable for framing and will state the number of shares purchased and the amount of each share, as well as the recipient's name. The home that you participate in "building" will last for many years and will continue to grow in value.

Here is a sample SHARE certificate:

YES, I WOULD LIKE TO HELP!

*I support the work that Habitat for Humanity does and I want to be part of the excitement! As a donor, I will receive periodic updates on your construction activities but, more importantly, I know my gift will help a family in our community realize the dream of homeownership. **I would like to SHARE in your efforts against substandard housing in my community!** (Please print below)*

PLEASE SEND ME _____ SHARES at $54.17 EACH = $ $_____

In Honor Of: _____

Occasion: (Circle One)   HOLIDAY   BIRTHDAY   ANNIVERSARY

      OTHER: _____

Address of Recipient: _____

Gift From: _____   *Donor Address:* _____

Donor Email: _____

I AM ENCLOSING A CHECK FOR $ $_____ PAYABLE TO HABITAT FOR HUMANITY <u>OR</u> PLEASE CHARGE MY VISA OR MASTERCARD *(CIRCLE ONE)*

Card Number _____ Expiration Date: _____

Name as it appears on Credit Card _____ Charge Amount $ _____

Signature _____

Billing Address _____

Telephone # Day _____ Eve _____

PLEASE NOTE: Your contribution is tax-deductible to the fullest extent allowed by law.
Habitat for Humanity • P.O. Box 1443 • Newport News, VA 23601 • 757-596-5553
www.HelpHabitatforHumanity.org

CPSIA information can be obtained at www.ICGtesting.com
Printed in the USA
BVOW031416120613

323146BV00001B/53/P